C000108213

Companion to
THE CYCLIST'S TRAINING BIBLE
3rd edition

Joe Friel

Boulder, Colorado

Copyright © 2009 by Joe Friel
All rights reserved. Printed in the USA.

No part of this book may be reproduced, stored in a retrieval system, or transmitted, in any form or by any means, electronic or photocopy or otherwise, without the prior written permission of the publisher except in the case of brief quotations within critical articles and reviews.

1830 55th Street
Boulder, Colorado 80301-2700 USA
303/440-0601 · Fax 303/444-6788 · E-mail velopress@competitorgroup.com

Distributed in the United States and Canada by Publishers Group West

Library of Congress Cataloging-in-Publication Data
Friel, Joe.
Companion to the cyclist's training bible / Joe Friel.—3rd ed.
    p. cm.
ISBN 978-1-934030-35-6 (pbk. : alk. paper)
1. Cycling—Training. I. Title.
GV1048.F748 2009
796.607—dc22

                                        2009016158

For information on purchasing VeloPress books, please call 800/234-8356
or visit www.velopress.com.

Cover design by Ryan Scheife, Mayfly Design
Interior design by Erin Johnson

Illustrations by Charlie Layton, pp. 28, 75, 83

09 10 11 / 10 9 8 7 6 5 4 3 2 1

Contents

Note: Chapter 13 (Stretching) does not include any new material, so it does not appear in this *Companion*.

Prologue to the 3rd Edition Companion

It's been fourteen years since I wrote *The Cyclist's Training Bible*. During that time a lot has changed, which has prompted me to revisit the book. Most of the changes are additions, and so it has grown considerably larger, just as the sport has grown. When I first sat down to write *The Cyclist's Training Bible* in 1995, road cycling was in decline and mountain biking was all the rage. Now road cycling is experiencing a rebirth.

This growth has caused the sport to change in other ways. In 1995 the average cyclist was more knowledgeable when it came to training, nutrition, equipment, and racing. Of course, at the time there was a lot less information to be aware of. In the past decade there has been an explosion of both training information and training technology. Power meters were pretty much unheard of in 1995. GPS devices for bikes had not been invented. And training software existed only in our imaginations.

Our knowledge of every aspect of training has grown. Physiology and nutrition have led the way, with sports psychology lagging slightly behind. As a result, how we should train and eat are much better defined than in 1995. But I'm afraid a result of this explosion of information and technology is that road racers are more confused than ever. That's why I felt a need to revise *The Cyclist's Training Bible.*

I've grown as a coach in the past fourteen years. Back then I could keep up with almost every new development that came down the pike—wheels, frame materials, sports nutrition products, helmets, bike fitting, skill techniques, races, web sites, books, and on and on. Now I find that it's impossible to stay abreast of everything. I have to focus my attention on a few topics, the ones that I find to be most important. As a result, I know a lot more about fewer things. I've tried to describe these things in the latest edition.

Although every chapter of the *Training Bible* except Chapter 13 (stretching) has new material, most additions have been in the chapters devoted to the intensity of training (Chapter 4), case studies (Chapter 11), strength (Chapter 12), and nutrition (Chapter 16). This *Companion* volume includes all of these additions to make it easy for you to find what is new if you own and have already read the third edition of *The Cyclist's Training Bible*. I suggest that while reading this *Companion* you keep your third edition close by so you can refer to it to refresh your memory from time to time. You'll find cross-references in the margins of this book to tell you where to find the background on more complicated concepts in the third edition.

You can use the cross-references provided to refresh your memory regarding more complicated concepts. You'll find page numbers cited in the margins of the text.

CYCLIST'S
TRAINING BIBLE
3rd ed.

See p. "x"

The *Companion* does not include the edits or clarifications that seem to always be necessary when revising a book. While these are minor changes, they are found only in the fourth edition, along with the additions included here. You can also go to my web site, trainingbible.com, or to my blog, trainingbible.com/joesblog/blog.html, for ongoing updates to much of the information found here.

As always, I hope my book proves helpful to your pursuit of the bicycle racing lifestyle. If it does (or even if it doesn't), feel free to e-mail me at jfriel@trainingbible.com and tell me about it. I attend many races throughout the season and would enjoy talking with you about your experiences. Hearing from those who benefit from my books is always a great pleasure and gives meaning to what is otherwise a solitary and tedious activity.

I wish you all the best for your training and racing!

Joe Friel
Scottsdale, Arizona

Acknowledgments

I am indebted, as always, to the athletes who have read *The Cyclist's Training Bible* and given me their suggestions for making it a more useful tool.

I also want to thank the staff at VeloPress, my publisher, who have continued to support my ideas for books and create products that get better every year. Special thanks go to Renee Jardine, associate publisher, for continuing to support my writing projects and for asking questions that the reader may want answered. Thanks also to Dave Trendler, marketing manager, for getting the word out whenever I give a training bible–based talk.

Nate Koch, P.T., A.T.C., director of rehabilitation at Endurance Rehabilitation in Scottsdale, Arizona, who assesses all of my coaching clients, reviewed the section in Chapter 5 on physical assessment and offered excellent suggestions. Thanks, Nate.

And, of course, thanks to my loving wife, Joyce, who after 41 years of marriage continues to support my passion for sport science by putting up with my 4 a.m. writing sessions and late evenings at the computer. Thanks, sweetheart.

1: Commitment

We all know that success in cycling begins with a passion for cycling. When you love to ride, the demands of training are much easier to accommodate. But commitment usually entails some kind of sacrifice. Even if you love to ride, if you stick with this sport long enough it will eventually require that you reach beyond what is easy or natural for you to pursue the next level of performance. It will test your limits—both your athletic abilities and your mind—but it can also be an exhilarating experience.

DEDICATION TO IMPROVEMENT

Lance Armstrong, Tiger Woods, and Michael Jordan are often referred to as being the greatest athletes of all time in their respective sports. What separates a good athlete from a world-class champion? Is it genetics or opportunity? Nature or nurture? Technique or mental toughness? What we've learned is that it is likely a focus on continual improvement.

Lance Armstrong is a legendary example of constant hard work. He is well known for keeping up a schedule of daily six-hour rides, repeatedly practicing key routes of the Tour de France, and weighing every bite of food that went into his mouth.

After Tiger Woods won the 1997 Masters Tournament by a record 12 strokes over the second-place finisher, he took time off from the sport in order to improve his swing. After becoming the only man to win the four major tournaments on the PGA Tour in succession, he again went back to work on improving his swing. In doing so, he has single-handedly changed the work ethic among pro golfers.

Being cut from his junior high school basketball team stiffened Michael Jordan's resolve to prove himself. Even after achieving athletic success, however, he was never one to rest on his laurels. He was well known among basketball fans for staying after practice to work on his "weaknesses."

What separates a good athlete from a world-class champion? It is likely a focus on continual improvement.

We know that constant dedication to improvement was critical to the success of each of these athletes. But was it the primary reason they became great? Recent research seems to indicate that it was. This research goes even further, suggesting that it takes ten years of focused work on one's sport to reach the threshold of greatness. That is certainly true for these three athletes. The high level of commitment that they have exhibited provides a model for other athletes hoping to achieve top ranking in their sport.

As a coach for the past three decades, I have found that the research about the length of time required for proficiency applies to cycling. The athlete improves physiologically for about seven years: During this time, athletes learn what it takes, in terms of training, racing, and lifestyle, to succeed in the sport. Then I see continued improvement in performance for at least another three years. This timeline holds true regardless of the age at which the athlete starts training and competing. Armstrong won the Iron Kids Triathlon at age 13 and nine years later was crowned the world road champion in cycling. At age 8 Woods took his first big win in the Optimist International Junior Championship, which he won five more times. His victory at the 1997 Masters came 13 years later, at age 21. After being cut from the basketball team, Jordan began to train and practice rigorously and at age 16 was the leading scorer on his high school team. It wasn't until nine years later, when he was playing with the Chicago Bulls, that he was named the most valuable player in the NBA.

MENTAL TOUGHNESS

Success in cycling requires an enormous amount of hard work physically—but the key to sustaining this level of work over many years is more mental than physical. Being mentally tough is what eventually produces high-level performance in athletes once they have achieved their physiological peak. What does it take to be mentally tough? There are four qualities I look for in athletes who say they want to perform at the highest levels: a desire to succeed, self-discipline, an attitude of believing in themselves, and patience (or perseverance). To evaluate whether you possess these qualities, ask yourself the questions that I ask athletes, which are included below.

Desire to Succeed

- Can you train alone, or do you need to be with others to motivate you to complete hard sessions?
- Do you find a way to work out regardless of environmental conditions such as rain, snow, wind, heat, darkness, or other potential training interruptions?

I find that athletes who regularly train alone tend to have higher levels of mental toughness. Likewise, those who ride in the rain and cold, or who find a way to regularly train despite busy work schedules and family commitments, reach levels of success that elude those who do not take their training that far.

Discipline

- Do you shape your training and lifestyle to fit your goals?
- How important to you are nutrition, sleep, periodization, goal setting, physical skills, attitude, health, and strength?
- Do your family and friends support you and your goals?

There are athletes who fit training into their lives as much as possible, and those for whom the daily ride is paramount and nearly everything else is secondary. I look for athletes who make workouts, diet, and rest a regular and reliable part of daily life. When those athletes are surrounded by a good support network, they're most likely to stick with a training program.

Belief in Self

- Do you go into a race with a success plan?
- Do you really believe you can succeed even when the conditions are not favorable?

- When it comes to racing, which do you think more about—the controllable or the uncontrollable variables?
- Do you accept occasional setbacks as necessary steps on the way to success or as signs you simply can't do it?
- Do you believe you can or question whether you can?

I've seen gifted athletes who didn't believe in their own potential, and I've seen those athletes defeated by physically weaker but mentally tougher competitors. If you don't truly believe that you can improve and win, it will be difficult for a coach to convince you otherwise.

Patience and Perseverance

- Are you in this for the long term?
- Do you need immediate success, or can you postpone it until the time is right, even if that is years in the future?
- Do you ever skip training for days or even weeks at a time and then try to get into shape quickly?

As discussed earlier, athletes continue to improve physiologically for about ten years, no matter what age they start training. Training to win is a long-term commitment that may have periods of seemingly no progress. Athletes need the patience to work steadily through those periods, knowing that improvement will come later.

———————————

My experience has been that if any one of these mental toughness qualities is lacking, the athlete will not achieve his or her lofty career goals. Few athletes have high levels of all these qualities. I've only coached one athlete who I felt had exceptional overall mental toughness—Ryan Bolton. He became a Team USA Olympian in triathlon. What set him apart from the others I have coached was his exceptional confidence. I have never had an athlete who believed in himself as much as Ryan did, and that was what made the difference for him.

Mental toughness is perhaps where the nurturing part of the success equation is most evident. Some athletes seem to have internalized these qualities at an early age. Others haven't. What makes the difference? It is probably hundreds of seemingly insignificant interactions that take place on a daily basis from birth through the formative years, experiences that we don't exactly know how to identify or instill.

It is quite a challenge for an adult athlete to become mentally tougher, but it can be done. Here's one way. I ask the athletes I coach to perform a simple ritual every night when they go to bed. It takes about 10 minutes to fall asleep after the lights go out. There are no interruptions. There is no television, radio, or Internet. No one is trying to sell you anything. This is the one time in the day when you are alone with only your thoughts. Take advantage of this peace and quiet to run a mental checklist of how you did in that day's training. Ask yourself: *Did I feel a strong desire to succeed today? Was I disciplined? Was I confident? Was I patient?* Look only for small victories. Don't dwell on setbacks. Success begets success. Do this every night and notice how it changes your outlook on life.

There are other ways to become mentally tougher. The best way to improve mental toughness is to work with a sports psychologist in much the same way as you would work with a coach. Sports psychology is a rapidly growing field, and it is becoming increasingly common for athletes at all competitive levels to seek the services of such professionals. Unfortunately, we tend to believe that athletes who seek help from a psychologist are mentally weak. But we see nothing wrong with their working with a coach to become more physically fit, and sports psychology is no different. However, finding a good sports psychologist is even more difficult than finding a coach. A starting place is often with a large coaching company that may have a close relationship with someone in this field. Ask at local bike shops or at a good health club. Just as with coaches, you will find that sports psychologists offer a wide range of services, fees, and ways of delivering their services. Shop around. The person you work with doesn't have to be local.

While you may not have been born to be a champion athlete—few people were—you have within you the capacity to perform at a much higher level than you have been willing to admit. It will take hard work, both mental and physical, to perform at close to your potential. I can help you with the physical part. Let's get started by training smarter than you have in the past.

2: Smart Training

Good training needs to be systematic and consistent. When you take the time to develop a successful training philosophy and evaluate your progress regularly, you reinforce both goals. Many of my "10 Commandments" for training also reflect these principles, and even the most successful cyclists can benefit from revisiting these dos and don'ts. Chances are, your years of cycling experience explain the rationale behind these rules. I know this is true for me.

CYCLIST'S
TRAINING BIBLE
3rd ed.

See pp. 12–18 for The 10 Commandments of Training

10 LESSONS FOR SMARTER TRAINING

I was once asked to talk about the most important lessons I had learned in nearly three decades of coaching. It was a good exercise as it ultimately helped me to review my coaching philosophy and highlight the key points. As I prepared my list, it became apparent that the essential lessons of smart training were really quite basic. Here is a list of what I think are the most important lessons for success as a cyclist.

Lesson 1: Have a clear goal. Most athletes think they have goals. Few really do. What most call goals are actually wishes—vague desires for grand achievements that are poorly defined. These often include the word "faster." When first starting a coaching program for an athlete, I generally have to help him or her define goals by asking questions such as *How much? When? Where? Is it a good stretch for you? Is it realistic?* Another good question to ask in order to better define an athlete's goals is *How will you know if this* *season was successful?* I also like to have the athlete set long-term objectives such as *What is the greatest accomplishment you'd like to achieve as a cyclist?* These really are dreams, but long-term dreams can eventually become goals. Knowing precisely what you want is critical to success in cycling, just as it is in life. Goal setting is discussed in greater detail in Chapter 8.

> Knowing precisely what you want is critical to success in cycling, just as it is in life.

Lesson 2: Determine what stands between you and your goal. If you set a goal at the start of the season and know you can achieve it even before setting out to train for it, then it wasn't much of a goal, was it? The idea of a goal is to have something for which you are striving that will cause you to become a better athlete. A good goal will stretch your limits. Since you don't believe you are currently capable of achieving that goal, there is obviously something standing between you and success, something you are lacking. Whatever this "something" may be is critical to your success. Instead of training randomly doing what you've done in the past, what your training partners want to do, or the workouts you read some pro does, you should isolate and improve this quality you are lacking and need for success. I call this "fixing the limiters." You'll find more on this subject in Chapter 6.

Lesson 3: Planning is necessary to achieve big goals. This may sound boring, but planning is at the heart of training, especially when your goals are big ones. I know you may have heard good athletes say they don't plan and do quite well anyway. I'd wager they really are following a plan, only it's not in writing—it's in their heads. Good athletes don't become good by training randomly. You won't either. The *Training Bible* is essentially about planning. Chapter 8 provides the details on how I lay out a seasonal plan for an athlete. Chapter 9 covers workout planning, and Chapter 10 discusses stage race planning.

Lesson 4: Measure progress toward your goals. There's nothing worse than thinking you are making good progress toward achieving your goal and finding out on race day that you are not physically ready. Had you known earlier that you weren't improving as expected in some aspect of fitness, you might have had time to correct the problem by changing your training. There are many ways to assess fitness progress. Chapter 5 addresses some of these.

Lesson 5: Do the least amount of training necessary to achieve your goal. This topic has already been discussed in my "10 Commandments" for training, but it is so important that it is worth repeating. When I was a much younger athlete, I thought my success depended on doing as much training as possible. What that led to was frequent injury, overtraining, illness, and burnout. It took me many years to figure out what I should be doing—only the training that is necessary to achieve my goals. Once I cut out the excess, I got better as an athlete. I've found it works the same way for those I coach. This theme of identifying what is important and then doing only that is carried throughout this book.

Lesson 6: Mental fitness is as important as physical fitness. Chapter 1 discusses mental toughness. I believe the key mental skill is confidence. Of all of the factors I consider when talking to an athlete I may coach, this is the most important. What I look for is a quiet "can-do" attitude. This is the common denominator for the best athletes I have known. A great deal of self-doubt is a sure sign of someone who is incapable of achieving high goals regardless of their physical ability.

Lesson 7: Skill is critical to athletic success. In endurance sports, with the possible exception of swimming, athletes tend to downplay or even disregard movement skills. Most athletes, especially those in the first three years in the sport, have lots of room for improvement of their sport-specific skills—balance, cornering, pedaling, and bike handling. As skills improve, less energy is wasted, meaning you can go faster for the same effort. You become more economical. Skills and economy for those new to the sport are discussed in Chapter 14.

Lesson 8: Train for the unique demands of the goal race. Every race is unique. The principal factor is race duration. There are many differences in training for a 40 km time trial, a 45-minute criterium, or a 60-mile road race. Beyond this are course profiles such as hilly, rolling, or flat; windy or calm conditions; hot and cold temperatures; courses with lots of or very few turns; off-road and road courses; morning and afternoon start times; and a multitude of other variables. Your training as you get closer to the race should take on more and more of its unique characteristics. In Chapter 10 you will learn how to write a race plan that takes into consideration the key variables over which you have control and how to deal with those you can't control.

Lesson 9: Recovery is just as important as hard workouts. Training is composed of two elements—hard work and recovery. One without the other makes for an ineffective program. I've found that most athletes have no problem with the hard work part. In fact, they seem to thrive on it. Where most need help is with recovery. Left to their own devices most cyclists will work too hard and rest too little. And since it is during rest that the body adapts and becomes fitter, training overly hard and resting too little is counterproductive. Chapter 18 takes a closer look at the details of recovery.

Lesson 10: Focus your lifestyle on success. The bigger your athletic goals are relative to your abilities, the more things in your life must be focused on achieving your goals. If your goal is to finish with the field in a local, short road race, you can afford to be a bit sloppy with nutrition, sleep, stress, training partners, friends, stretching, equipment, workout analysis, and strength work—and still do well. But if your goal is to win the race or make it to the podium at a national championship, you will need to get everything in your life pointed at cycling success. Since the people who ask me to coach them are aimed at such big goals, I spend a lot of time helping them focus their lifestyles on success. Chapters 15 through 18 address most of these issues.

One last bit of advice. Have fun. This may seem obvious, but some athletes are so focused on achieving the right numbers in their logs that they've forgotten why they got involved in the sport in the first place. They've taken the fun out of it. Many of the pros I talk to are amazed at how much training time age groupers do on top of working 50 to 60 hours per week, raising a couple of kids, getting them to soccer practice, taking care of the landscaping, doing volunteer work and myriad other responsibilities. By comparison, the pros have it easy; they just train 30 to 40 hours per week with a few naps sprinkled in. But they also tell me that if it ever stops being fun they will quit racing and get a real job. Fun is the reason each of us participates in cycling. You're probably not earning a living riding a bike—never lose sight of that. You are not defined by your most recent race result. Your kids won't love you any less if you have a "bad" race. The sun will still come up tomorrow. Smile more and frown less. You will enjoy cycling more and do better in the sport because of it.

3: The Science of Training

How can we measure physical fitness? Science has discovered four of its most basic components—aerobic capacity, lactate threshold, aerobic threshold, and economy. The top riders have excellent values for all four of these physiological traits.

In the *Training Bible* you read about lactate threshold, sometimes called the "anaerobic threshold." This is a critical intensity level for the cyclist, especially one who focuses on doing short and fast races. The ability to go long and hard near and above the lactate threshold is the determiner in who makes the selection in hotly contested racing. The other critical threshold for cyclists racing at all distances is the "aerobic threshold."

CYCLIST'S
TRAINING BIBLE
3rd ed.

See pp. 21–23 for more on Aerobic Capacity, Lactate Threshold, and Economy

AEROBIC THRESHOLD

Aerobic threshold occurs at a much lower intensity than lactate threshold but is just as critical to race success. Riding at your aerobic threshold is about the intensity at which the peloton travels. Having excellent aerobic fitness allows you to ride easily in the peloton for hours, if necessary, and still be fresh and ready when race tactics call for a great effort—for a match to be burned, in other words.

The aerobic threshold cannot be pinpointed in a lab, but it is physiologically marked by a slight increase in the depth of breathing accompanied by a sense of moderate-effort intensity. In terms of heart rate, it occurs in zone 2 (heart rate training zones are described in Chapter 4 of the *Training*

Bible). For those in great shape, power output will be quite high at this heart rate. The aerobic threshold will also vary from day to day based on how well rested you are. As with the lactate threshold, when you are fresh it will be found at a higher power output than when you are fatigued.

When it comes to the aerobic threshold, paying close attention to your effort is just as important as watching your heart rate monitor or power meter.

Intensity at the lactate threshold is so great that fatigue may well prevent you from achieving an excessively high heart rate. That is not the case with the much lower-intensity aerobic threshold. Because of high motivation, you may push yourself too hard when fatigued during an aerobic threshold workout. So when it comes to the aerobic threshold, paying close attention to your effort is just as important as watching your heart rate monitor or power meter.

Training in the aerobic threshold zone is perfect for building basic aerobic endurance, which is a primary focus during the Base training period. For this reason, a good portion of each week's training in the Base period should be devoted to training at the aerobic threshold. You'll find some rides to measure your aerobic threshold in *Companion* Chapter 4.

4: Intensity

Of the three basic elements of training—frequency, duration, and intensity—the most important element to get right is intensity. Oddly enough, this is the part cyclists all too often get wrong. Most train too intensely when they should be going easy. Then when it's time to go fast they are a little too tired to push their limits. As a result, all of their training becomes moderate. They race the same way: Stay with the pack until it's time to put the hammer down. Then they're off the back wondering how they got there.

Technology is providing increasingly better equipment to measure (and temper) intensity in training. Power meters are now readily available to cyclists and more affordable than ever. You might be contemplating whether you should buy a power meter.

MEASURING INTENSITY WITH POWER

If I was your coach you'd have to train with a power meter. I require every cyclist I work with to use one. Why do I do that? Because I know athletes are more likely to achieve their race goals by training—and racing—with power than without. I've seen it happen with every athlete I've coached.

Power meters are more valuable to the serious rider than a lighter frame or faster wheels. Given the choice, I'd recommend a power meter every time. Why? Let's start with a basic reason—getting the intensity right for workouts.

Power meters remove most of the guesswork that goes into training and racing. For example, I've known athletes who, when doing intervals with heart rate monitors, don't call the work interval "started" until their heart rates reach the targeted level. With a power meter you soon learn that the interval starts as soon as the power hits the targeted zone—which means right away. Training the heart is not the main objective of doing intervals—or any workout, for that matter. For most workouts, what happens in the muscles is really the key to your fitness and racing ability. Heart rate monitors, though quite valuable to training, have many believing that training is just about the heart. It isn't.

CYCLIST'S
TRAINING BIBLE
3rd ed.

See pp. 40–42 and 44–48 for more on RPE and heart rate monitors

Don't get me wrong, heart rate monitors are great training devices, too. They are another tool I require my athletes to use. In fact, heart rate monitors are even more beneficial now that there are power meters. Before we began measuring intensity in terms of power, you could only compare heart rate to how you felt, or Rate of Perceived Exertion (RPE). Having power for comparison makes the heart rate information much more valuable because power output is objective.

Also, with only a heart rate monitor, how do you get the intensity right in the first minute or so of the first few intervals in a workout? Heart rate certainly can't be relied on then, as it is low at that point and still rising for the first couple of minutes. Are you riding too hard or too easy? How do you know? A power meter tells you precisely, and right away.

Using a power meter in a time trial is almost like cheating. When everyone else is fighting the wind, or flying downwind, or guessing how hard to go when climbing, the rider with a power meter is just rolling along at the prescribed power. He or she will produce the fastest possible time given the conditions so long as the optimal target power has been determined through training and observed closely during the race. Although something similar can be done with heart rate, there are some confounding factors, such as cardiac drift, the acute effect of diet, and the slow response on hills, that make heart rate monitors less than optimal as training tools.

> Using a power meter in a time trial is almost like cheating. . . . The rider with a power meter is just rolling along at the prescribed power.

Power meters also provide highly accurate details about how your fitness is changing throughout the season. I test the athletes I coach regularly using a combination of heart rate and power. This testing procedure is described later in this chapter (see "Assessing Aerobic Threshold"). Without this information I really wouldn't know for sure whether they were making progress. I might think they were, based on other observations, but I'd just be guessing. With a power meter I know exactly how much progress each athlete has made.

There are many benefits of training with power. Perhaps the best indicator of their value for performance is the elite athletes who use them. Power meters are common with professional road cyclists—and for an obvious reason: They have mortgages to pay, and a power meter will help them do that.

As we discussed in the *Training Bible*, power-based training begins with determining your critical power profile at various distances. To review, you can define your critical power profile with four time trials of 1, 6, 12, and 30 minutes. Each test is a maximum effort for the entire duration. It's important that you be rested for the critical power tests, so it's best to conduct the tests over several days.

CYCLIST'S
TRAINING BIBLE
3rd ed.

See pp. 60–61 for more on Critical Power Tests

To estimate 60-minute power, subtract 5 percent from your 30-minute average power result. Once you've established your critical power for 60 minutes (CP60), you can use it as the basis for your power training zones. Table 1 shows you how to do this using the system created by Hunter Allen and Andy Coggan and described in their book *Training and Racing with a Power Meter*.

TABLE 1: Power Zones Based on CP60

ZONE 1	ZONE 2	ZONE 3	ZONE 4	ZONE 5	ZONE 6	ZONE 7
Recovery	Aerobic	Tempo	Threshold	Aerobic capacity	Anaerobic capacity	Power
<56%	56–75%	76–90%	91–105%	106–120%	121–150%	>150%

TRAINING TIME BY INTENSITY ZONE

How much time should you spend in each heart rate or power zone over the course of a season? This is a question often asked by cyclists, and with good reason. The answer would tell you exactly what you needed to know to design a program of purposeful and effective training. Unfortunately, it's not an easy question to answer.

FIGURE 1: Time Trial Periodization

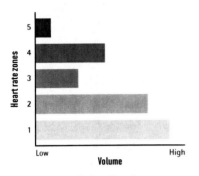

Relative distribution of intensity over the course of a season when training for 30- to 90-minute bicycle time trials.

FIGURE 2: Criterium Periodization

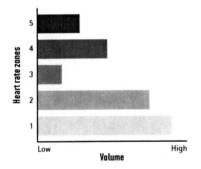

Relative distribution of intensity over the course of a season when training for bicycle criterium-type races lasting 30–90 minutes.

FIGURE 3: Road Race Periodization

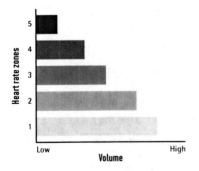

Relative distribution of intensity over the course of a season when training for bicycle road races lasting 90 minutes to 6 hours.

Training intensity is determined by many variables, the most important being the event for which you are training. There are significant differences between preparing for a 40 km time trial and a criterium. Preparing for a 40 km time trial requires a lot of steady training just below and at the lactate threshold, but for a short criterium a great deal of interval work is done above the lactate threshold. Obviously one cannot train in the same way for both events.

It's not really possible to say how much time most athletes should spend in each zone over the course of the season because every athlete is different. There is no generic "cyclist" and no perfect one-size-fits-all training plan. There are differences in the types of races each athlete does, differences in their limiters, and differences in their race priorities. But let's take a stab at mapping out a very general estimate.

Figures 1 through 3 suggest what training time by heart rate zone for an entire season might look like, assuming that a given type of race is always an A-priority. The purpose of these figures is not to give you specific numbers or volumes to shoot for, but rather to suggest how training intensity might generally be distributed. The examples might serve as a rough guide for you as you make decisions about how many low-intensity and high-intensity workouts to schedule in your training.

ASSESSING AEROBIC THRESHOLD

To test aerobic threshold, we'll pull together some of the intensity concepts I've already introduced—aerobic threshold, heart rate, and power.

For the serious rider, it is important to know when enough aerobic threshold training has been done to establish a good base for the bottom of the fitness pyramid. To figure this out, look at heart rate and power to see if the two are staying closely linked, with little or no cardiac drift. Cardiac drift is the tendency of the heart rate to rise even though power remains steady, and in an aerobically fit athlete it is minimal.

The following explains an advanced method that you may use to determine whether aerobic fitness is as good as it should be near the end of the Base period. This is a number-crunching exercise that requires a power meter and WKO+ software (available from TrainingPeaks.com).

On a bike with a power meter, complete an aerobic threshold ride (as detailed in the "Aerobic Threshold Rides" sidebar). Then upload the power meter's heart rate and power data to the WKO+ analysis software. The software will separate the aerobic threshold portion of the ride into two halves. For each half, the average power is divided by the average heart rate to establish a ratio. The results are then compared by subtracting the first half ratio from the second half ratio and dividing the remainder by the first half ratio. This produces a power-to-heart-rate ratio percentage of change from the first half to the second half of the aerobic threshold ride. Don't worry,

Aerobic Threshold Rides

There are two ways to do an aerobic threshold coupling workout. You can ride while keeping heart rate steady to see what happens to power. Or you can maintain a steady power output and see what heart rate does. In the Base period, it's generally better to maintain a steady heart rate, while for the Build period you should keep power steady.

In the early Base period, you should start these aerobic threshold rides at 20 to 30 minutes and then increase them weekly. Do two of these each week during Base. When you can do an aerobic threshold ride for two hours while your heart rate and power remain coupled, you can consider your aerobic threshold fitness fully developed. Congratulations! Your primary goal of the Base period has been accomplished. Assuming your force and speed skills are also well advanced, you are now ready to move on to more advanced goals such as building muscular endurance, anaerobic endurance, and power. In the Build period, you will need to maintain your endurance by doing an aerobic threshold ride about every two weeks.

the software will do all of this calculating for you. But just so you under-stand the concept, here is an example of how power-to-heart-rate ratio per-centage of change is calculated:

First half of aerobic threshold portion of ride:
Power average: 180 watts
Heart rate average: 135 bpm
First half power-to-heart-rate ratio (180/135): 1.33

Second half of aerobic threshold portion of ride:
Power average: 178 watts
Heart rate average: 139 bpm
Second half power-to-heart-rate ratio (178/139): 1.28

Calculating change:
First half ratio minus second half ratio (1.33 − 1.28): 0.05
Remainder divided by the first half ratio (0.05/1.33): 0.038
Power-to-heart-rate shift: 3.8 percent

If your power-to-heart-rate shift is less than 5 percent, as in the above example, the workout is said to be "coupled," meaning the power and heart

FIGURE 4: Coupled Aerobic Threshold Workout

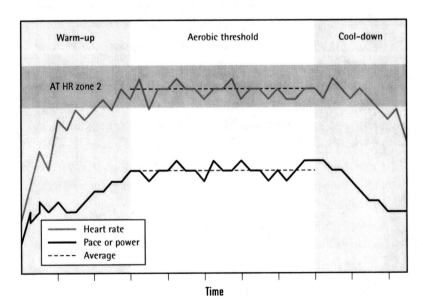

FIGURE 5: Decoupled Aerobic Threshold Workout

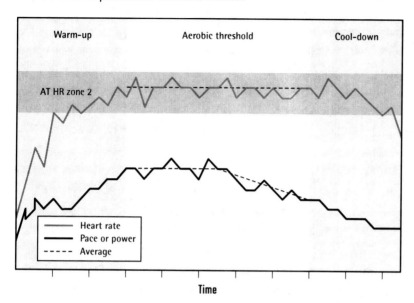

rate graph lines stay close to parallel, as shown in Figure 4. That's good: It means that you have a low level of cardiac drift. But if the power-to-heart-rate ratio shift is greater than 5 percent, the workout is "decoupled," as shown in Figure 5. Note that the two lines on this graph do not remain parallel for the entire aerobic threshold portion of the workout. That level of cardiac drift indicates that you have a low level of Base period fitness.

If you don't have a power meter, you can still do aerobic threshold workouts using your trusty heart rate monitor. You will have to make decisions about your aerobic endurance fitness based strictly on perceived exertion. Over time, the effort at aerobic threshold heart rate will seem to be getting easier, and you should find yourself riding faster over the same course at the same heart rate.

USING SOFTWARE TO MEASURE FORM, FITNESS, AND FATIGUE

Although discussion in *The Cyclist's Training Bible* on the topic of periodization sounds very scientific, measuring its results have largely been a leap of faith. Coaches and athletes have simply trusted that organizing workouts in a certain way produces peak readiness on race day. During training it has always been possible to take "snapshots" of your fitness every four weeks or so by doing aerobic or lactate threshold tests. But since the physiological changes are generally quite small—on the order of 1 percent—variables such as weather, the warm-up, and even a few cups of coffee can easily make it appear that there was either great progress or none over the previous few weeks. So you are back to trusting your instincts about whether you are becoming fitter.

Now all of that is changing. With power meters and new software designed by Hunter Allen and Andrew Coggan, it is possible to graph and manage the daily changes in your race preparation. The software is called WKO+ and is compatible with all power meters on the market as of 2008.

One of the most powerful features of WKO+ is its performance management chart, which allows you to track periodization and progress toward your race goals. Figure 6 is based on this chart for the early season for one of the athletes I coach. This is a good example of the future of training technology. If you are serious about your race performance, such software will allow you to keep a close eye on your progress and respond quickly when small periodization changes are necessary to stay on track toward your goals.

FIGURE 6: Performance Chart for Sample Athlete

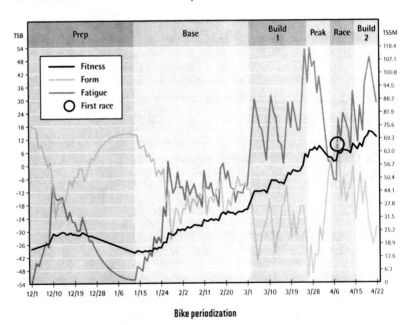

Bike periodization

There are three aspects of training represented by the lines on Figure 6. All are derived from formulas determined by certain power-based variables—normalized power, intensity factor, and Training Stress Score. (To learn more about these details, see Allen and Coggan's book, *Training and Racing with a Power Meter*.) These variables reflect the intensity, duration, and frequency of your bike workouts. Collectively, we can use this information to anticipate performance and better time intensity in training.

The dark gray line on Figure 6 represents *fatigue*. It closely approximates what you would subjectively describe after a few days of hard training, and it responds very quickly to high and low levels of training stress. Notice the spikes and valleys. These indicate alternating hard and easy workout days. The spikes show increased training stress from long duration or high intensity as well as the frequency of such workouts. The valleys represent short, easy rides or days off the bike.

The solid black line is for *fitness*. When this line rises, fitness is improving. Relative to fatigue, fitness responds slowly to training stress. Notice that it isn't a straight line. Fitness is never static; it is always changing, either positively or negatively. Also, fitness only increases after an earlier increase in fatigue. Fitness and fatigue go hand in hand. This makes sense, as being fatigued means you trained hard, and hard training produces greater fitness. Although a few days of extended rest are necessary every three or four weeks to prevent overtraining and burnout, you must be careful not to make the break too long, or too much fitness will be lost. The software allows you to monitor these changes. Effectively balancing rest and stress is tricky when it comes to fitness.

The lighter gray line on Figure 6 represents *form*, which may also be described as race "restedness." This use of the word "form" comes from late-nineteenth-century British horse racing when bettors would review a page of previous race results for the horses in that day's race—a form. A horse was said to be "on form" when racing well. Cycling adopted the term.

Form rises when you back off from hard training to rest more. It falls when you train frequently with high-intensity or long workouts. On the left side of the graph, you see a 0 (zero) in the center of the scale. When the black line is above this "horizontal zero" point, the athlete is "on form."

So now let's take a look at my athlete's early-season periodization and see how it worked out. Along the fitness curve, I've indicated his early-season periods: Prep, Base, Build 1, Peak, and Race. The second Build period following the Race period is the start of his return to hard training in preparation for the next A-priority race on his schedule.

As described earlier, the Prep period is a time when the athlete is just getting back into training following a break at the end of the previous season. In this case, it was December through early January. He had a family vacation planned for the last three weeks of this period and did not have a bike available. Here, since he wasn't riding, you can see the steady drop in both fatigue and fitness. Accompanying that drop is a rise in form. He was really rested but, of course, his bike fitness was becoming increasingly poor.

In the Base period he returned to steady and consistent training. He spent time on the indoor trainer working on aerobic endurance, muscular force, and pedaling speed skills. The steady rise in fatigue and fitness with a drop in form all indicate that training was going as expected.

During the first Build period I began to increase the intensity of his training by including muscular endurance and anaerobic endurance rides. These consisted primarily of intervals and tempo rides while maintaining the three basic abilities he established during the Base period—endurance, force, and speed skills. Both fatigue and fitness rose at a greater rate, and form dropped to his lowest point of the early season because of this increase in the training load. I made slight adjustments to stress and rest along the way because the chart revealed how he was responding to training.

In the short Peak period, he did only a few hard workouts with lots of rest between them. Notice how fatigue dropped dramatically while fitness decreased only slightly. The most important change here is the rapid rise in form, which increased above the horizontal zero point mentioned above. At his first race he was not only at a high level of fitness, he was also well rested. This was confirmed by his perception of feeling ready on race day as well as by his exceptional race performance. He was *on form*.

Following this first race of the season, he went on a mountain-biking vacation for a few days and resumed hard training on his return. As you can see by where the graph ends, he was well on his way to the second peak of the season, which produced even better results.

Form, fitness, and fatigue cannot be perfectly timed for every race, but they can give you valuable insight on adjustments that need to be made to training intensity. If you decide not to use a power meter you can use your training diary and other workout data to follow patterns of fatigue and recovery.

5: Testing

At the end of every cycling season you should update your personal profile: Begin by ranking your performance within your race category, using a scale of 1 to 5. Then revisit your Natural Abilities Profile and your Mental Skills Profile. These are more subjective measures of your progress as a cyclist, but they are no less important. You will enjoy seeing how your competencies have developed and get a better sense of what to focus on in the coming season.

Yet another essential component making up a comprehensive personal assessment is the medical evaluation.

CYCLIST'S
TRAINING BIBLE
3rd ed.

See pp. 65–72 for more on personal profiles

MEDICAL EVALUATION

Before you start back into training for a new season, it's a good idea to have your doctor give you a complete physical exam. The older you become, the more important this is. It's most likely that nothing unusual will be found. Then again, your doctor may discover something important, such as skin cancer, high blood pressure, high cholesterol, or prostate or breast cancer. Conditions such as these are much easier to treat in their early stages than they are later on. Getting an annual physical exam is just a good preventative practice regardless of how active you are, but it is even more important for you as an athlete because you will be putting more stress on your body than the average person. Of course, your doctor will probably give you a clean bill of health. Then you are ready to take the next step.

The more fit you are, the less likely you are to believe there could ever be anything wrong with your health. Ask Lance Armstrong: At what he thought was the pinnacle of his career as a cyclist, after having won the world road championship, he discovered he had cancer. Health problems can happen to anyone, no matter how fit they are.

I also advise every athlete to make a preseason appointment with a physical therapist. Look for one who has experience working with endurance athletes. Some insurance plans allow you to go directly to a physical therapist without a doctor's prescription. If your health insurance does not cover such a visit to a physical therapy center, be prepared to pay for a costly one-hour screening (at least $100–200). What you will learn is well worth the cost.

The physical therapist will do a head-to-toe exam looking for potential injury sites due to lack of strength, limited flexibility, or physical imbalances. He or she can tell you how to modify your training to improve the condition or how to adjust equipment to allow for your unique weaknesses.

Getting an annual physical exam is just a good preventative practice, but it is even more important for you as an athlete because you will be putting more stress on your body than the average person.

We all have physical imperfections. You may discover that you have leg-length discrepancies, both functional and physical; weak core muscles that allow your body to be moved from side to side and rotated when it should be still; tight muscles and tendons; muscle imbalances; limited range of motion in your joints; poor posture; or scoliosis. These may be hereditary, caused by long-ago injury, or simply the result of the repetitive motions of riding a bike for many years. The physical therapist can suggest strengthening or stretching exercises to correct these imperfections.

The physical therapist may also wish to refer you to a bike-fit specialist. Although your bike shop may have measured you for a custom bike, a fit specialist will take that process several steps further by assessing your working position on the bike in some detail. This usually involves taking several laser measurements as you ride on a trainer. The specialist may recommend cleat spacers, shoe orthotics, slight changes in the bike's stem or crank length, or a special type of saddle.

LAB TESTING

At least once each year, generally in the early Base period, I send my athletes to the lab for metabolic testing, sometimes called gas analysis. Athletes usually refer to this as a "VO$_2$max test," but it goes well beyond discovering your VO$_2$max. Most think this test reveals their potential for high-level performance. It does not tell you this any more than competing in a race shows your potential for future races. But this test does quantify your current level of fitness from many different angles.

Metabolic testing assesses your current fitness level and can also provide useful information about heart rate zones, bike power zones, how much fat and how many carbohydrates you use at various intensities, and how efficient you are when pedaling a bike. Lab testing also helps to establish your personal rating of perceived exertion on a given scale (for example, a scale of 1 to 10, where 1 is easy and 10 is hard) so that you can think about effort more precisely in the future. All of this will help fine-tune your training plan.

That's a lot to be gained from one test session that takes only about an hour to complete. If you are self-coached, the technician can help you make sense of the test results and may even offer suggestions on how to use the information to train more effectively.

This can also be an investment of at least $100 to $200. Look for a facility that specializes in athlete testing, not one that caters to those at risk for heart disease or aging populations. Athlete testing centers are becoming increasingly available in bike shops, health clubs, and physical therapy centers. Some coaches even provide this service.

By repeating the test at the start of each major period of the season, especially the Base 1, Build 1, and Peak periods, you can closely monitor your training progress. These tests also serve as great motivators when you don't have a race scheduled for some time.

CYCLIST'S
TRAINING BIBLE
3rd ed.

*See pp. 54–61
for Performance
Assessment tests*

Throughout the season you should be assessing your fitness with the time trial and graded exercise tests found in Chapter 5 of the *Training Bible*. These tests provide a baseline at the start of each new season and milestones further down the road.

6: Racing Abilities

I n this chapter I discuss basic and advanced racing abilities. Speed skills are one of the most important basic racing abilities.

CYCLIST'S
TRAINING BIBLE
3rd ed.

*See pp. 75–77
for more on Basic
Racing Abilities*

SPEED SKILLS

Speed skills are the ability to move quickly and efficiently. Racers with strong speed skills can pedal smoothly at a high cadence and negotiate turns quickly without wasted movement. "Speed skills" is not used here as a synonym for velocity, although this is a related issue. As speed skills improve, so do race times and performances.

Cycling speed is affected by both cadence and gear size, as illustrated by the following formula:

$$\text{Bike speed} = \text{stroke rate} \times \text{gear size}$$

To ride a bike fast, you can either turn the pedals around at a high rate, use a high gear, or do a little of both. That's all there is to it.

Of course, in the real world of bike racing there's more to it than just that. We need to factor in aerobic capacity (VO_2max), lactate threshold, and economy of movement. These physiological markers of fitness make it possible to maintain a high cadence and big gear over time. Of these, the most highly trainable of these factors for the fit athlete is economy of movement—or pedaling in the world of cycling.

Economy of movement is defined as how much effort you use when pedaling at a given power output. The goal is to make quick movements with little wasted energy. By improving your economy you can go faster with the same effort. This is the ability I call "speed skills"—one of the critical corners of the training triad.

As with force, speed-skills training progresses from the general to the specific. The goal for this ability is to be able to pedal comfortably (in other words, with a lower energy expenditure) at a higher cadence than you are now capable of doing. Several scientific studies have demonstrated that leg turnover is trainable, given the right types of workouts and consistency of purpose. Such training will start with drills (general) and slowly move toward riding with a higher cadence than you currently employ (specific).

> **By improving your economy you can go faster with the same effort. This is the ability I call "speed skills."**

Good pedaling skills are based on a slight amount of "ankling" (see Figure 7). This means using your ankle like a movable hinge instead of a rigid crowbar. On flat terrain, during the upstroke the ankle slowly opens, allowing the heel to rise slightly above the toes (position H). On the downstroke the ankle closes a bit so that the heel is even with or slightly below the toes (position B). On a climb, ankling may be a bit more pronounced.

FIGURE 7: Pedaling Biomechanics: Foot Position and Resultant Force

An easy way to determine how economically you pedal is to simply see what the highest cadence is that you can maintain for several minutes in a low gear. Lance Armstrong proved to be a master at this during his Tour de France victory years, when he raced time trials at a remarkably high 110 to 120 rpm. When he first came onto the world cycling stage in the early 1990s, he was a "masher," turning the cranks at 80 to 90 rpm. By the late 1990s he had completely overhauled his pedaling mechanics to be much more economical—and more competitive as a result.

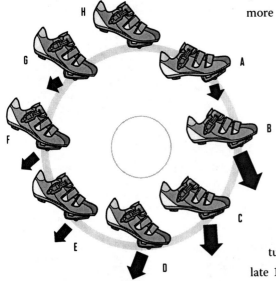

Adapted with permission from Cavanagh and Sanderson 1986.

Economy can be improved if you work at it. This will result in faster race times and better results, but it will take time to accomplish. One study using Swedish runners found that economy continued to improve 22 months after VO_2max had plateaued. It takes a long-term dedication, not just a brief experiment of only a few workouts.

Are you already so economical that further work is unnecessary? That's unlikely. In the early 1980s, American running legend Steve Scott improved his economy by a whopping 6 percent just before setting a world record for the mile. If an elite runner who already had excellent economy could improve by so much, what can the rest of us do? A 1 percent enhancement in pedaling economy could shave 30 to 40 seconds off of your 40 km time trial. What would a 6 or even a 10 percent improvement mean for your performance?

The downside of changing your biomechanics is that initially you will get slower or feel like you are working harder. This may last several weeks but will gradually turn around. When it does, you will go faster for the same level of effort. Hang in there until then.

7: Planning to Race

There are three elements of physical preparation to carefully balance over the course of your training—fatigue, fitness, and form. We touched on these elements in our discussion of how power meter software can provide better visibility of your performance potential (see *Companion* Chapter 5). While you may opt not to use power meter software to produce a performance chart, you still need to learn how to manage fluctuations in fatigue and fitness so you can race when your form is high.

Fatigue is a measure of how great your workload has been over the past few days. High-intensity and long-duration workouts produce fatigue and fitness simultaneously—hard training makes you tired and also makes you more fit. But fitness increases much more slowly than fatigue. Three hard workouts in three days will produce a lot of fatigue, but only a tiny increase in fitness. So fitness is best measured in weeks, whereas fatigue is measured in days.

Form has to do with how well rested you are. You can have high form (if you are well rested and have a low level of fatigue), but low fitness (if you have allowed yourself too much rest). The trick to preparing for a race is to reduce fatigue, maintain fitness or allow only a slight decrease, and increase form. So how do you achieve that ideal?

> To tap your greatest potential on race day, you'll want to see a dramatic decrease in fatigue in the days leading up to the race, while form rises steadily and fitness drops only slightly.

Fitness, fatigue, and form will fluctuate over the course of your training. The demands you place on yourself within each period of training will be easy to see when you track your fatigue. As intensity increases with a focus on muscular endurance and anaerobic endurance in the Build period, fatigue will build, culminating in race-intensity workouts in the Peak period. Consequently, form will suffer with so much fatigue, but in both the recovery weeks and the taper, form will bounce back thanks to the reduction in fatigue.

Your overall fitness should steadily increse over the course of the season, proving that your training is effective. You can refer back to the performance chart of one of my athletes for an example of how this happens in the real world (see Figure 6). To tap your greatest potential on race day, you'll want to see a dramatic decrease in fatigue in the days leading up to the race, while form rises steadily and fitness drops only slightly.

THE PEAKING PROCESS

Peaking consists of two to three weeks of short, race-intensity workouts that simulate the conditions of the race every third or fourth day. You can either use nearby races for these workouts, or follow the guidelines I've outlined below.

The intensity of the race simulation workouts is key to maintaining fitness while peaking. You should ride at maximum race level, *at least* power or heart rate zone 3, or a moderately hard perceived exertion. The workouts should get shorter as you progress through the Peak period. So, if you use the workouts provided, start with the longer durations and gradually reduce them with each succeeding workout. Your total weekly volume should also taper in order to incorporate more rest.

Allow more time for the Peak period if you are training for a longer race, if you have a particularly high fitness level, if you are injury prone, or if you are an older athlete.

Race-Intensity Workouts
Be sure to include a warm-up and cool-down in every workout.

Goal Race: Criterium
- On a criterium-style course do 15–30 sets, each a 10-second sprint out of corners. Do one set for every 3 minutes of race duration. (For

example, for a 45-minute criterium you would do 15 sprints and for a 90-minute race you would do 30.)

- Follow each sprint with a 20-second recovery, including an extra minute of rest after every fifth sprint.
- Reduce the number of sprints by three to five each time this workout is done during the Peak period.
- This workout is best done with training partners. Take turns leading.

Goal Race: Hilly Road Race

- Find a challenging hill similar to one in the race. Do hill repeats totaling 20 to 40 minutes at your target power level or heart rate, or at what feels like race intensity. Your total climbing time should equal the time you will spend climbing in the race.
- On each climb, once every 30 to 60 seconds, stand while shifting to a higher gear and accelerate for 12 pedal strokes.
- Recover after each climb for as long as it took to do the climb.
- Reduce the session's total climbing time by about 20 percent each time this workout is done during the Peak period.

Goal Race: Flat Road Race

- Start by riding in heart rate zones 3 to 5 (or CP90 to CP60 if using a power meter) for 20 to 40 minutes in a very aero position, alternating pulls with a training partner every 3 to 5 minutes. The rider pulling should briefly attempt to drop the other rider once in each pull. This should be when the trailing rider least expects it.
- Finish the workout by doing 6 to 8 maximum-effort 20-second sprints.
- Reduce the duration of the steady-state portion by about 20 percent each time you do this workout during the Peak period.

Goal Race: Time Trial

- On a time trial bike, do 20 to 40 minutes of total time, depending on the race length. Make the hard-effort portion of the workout about 60–70 percent of your anticipated race finish time.
- Do a series of intervals, each 4 to 8 minutes long at rate of perceived exertion, power, or heart rate. (For longer races, such as 40 km time trials, use longer intervals; for shorter races, use shorter intervals.)

- Follow each interval with a recovery that is one-fourth as long as the preceding work interval.
- Reduce the total interval time by about 20 percent for this session each time you do this workout during the Peak period.

The two or three days of easy workouts between race simulations are designed to erase fatigue and elevate form. A good Peak period balances intensity and rest so that you come into race readiness at the right time.

Race Week

The week of the race is a little different. Now you really want to emphasize rest but still need to do just a bit of intensity to maintain fitness. Long workouts are not at all necessary to maintain race fitness at this point. Do three or four workouts this week in which you complete several 90-second intervals at expected race intensity or at least zone 3 as described above, with three-minute recoveries. Five days before the race do five of these 90-second efforts. Four days before do four times 90 seconds. This pattern continues throughout the week. The easiest day of race week should be two days before the race. This is usually best as a day off but for the high-volume athlete it may be a short and easy ride. The day before should also include some race-like intensity within a very brief session. For example, ride 30 to 60 minutes, including a few short efforts at race intensity or higher.

Following this pattern in the last few weeks before important races will maintain your fitness, decrease your fatigue, and increase your form. You're peaked and ready to race.

PERIODIZATION ALTERNATIVES

📖
CYCLIST'S
TRAINING BIBLE
3rd ed.

*See pp. 92–100
for more on
Periodization*

If you've read *The Cyclist's Training Bible,* you are no stranger to the concept of periodization. If you've put it into practice in your own training, your year is divided into periods and in each period you focus on improving a specific aspect of your fitness while maintaining the gains made in previous periods. The peaking process is a good demonstration of this.

All of the training suggestions in this book are based on the linear periodization model. Although it is the one that is easiest to understand and has become the most common way of organizing the training season for endurance athletes, it is not the only periodization model. There are several models that are common in endurance sports.

Linear Periodization

Figure 8 illustrates what is known as the "linear" or "classic" periodization model. The season begins with a focus on training volume as you do long and frequent workouts at low intensity. This way of starting off the season creates a high level of aerobic endurance fitness while building injury resistance through low-intensity stress. Then, in the Build period, you decrease volume by doing long sessions less frequently, increasing the intensity of your training. This improves the advanced abilities of muscular endurance, anaerobic endurance, and power, as described in Chapter 6 of the *Training Bible*, as you get closer to the target race.

FIGURE 8: Linear (Classic) Periodization

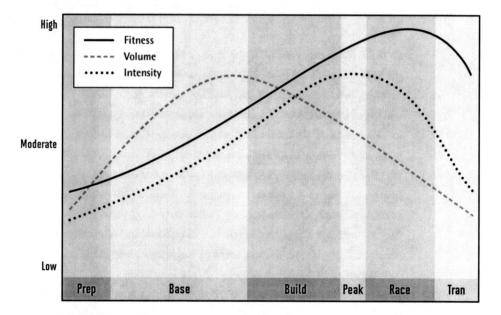

Undulating Periodization

Figure 9 shows one way the "undulating periodization model" may be employed. Essentially, volume and intensity are rising and falling alternately

FIGURE 9: Undulating Periodization

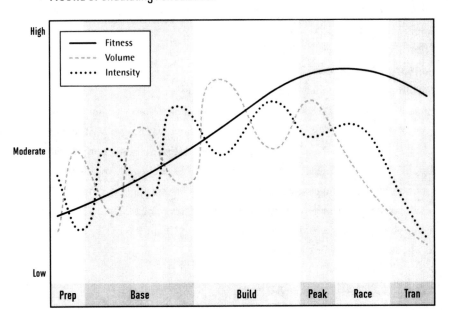

as the season progresses. In this way, undulating periodization changes the short-term focus to include more variety. A variation of this method involves rotating several of the abilities weekly. For example, you might work on endurance one day, anaerobic endurance a couple of days later, and force a couple of days after that, with recovery days in between. The next week may alternate muscular endurance, speed skills, and power.

Because the variety built into this model maintains motivation, I sometimes use it late in the season after general fitness is well established. It also works well with strength training in the early Base period by alternating the Anatomical Adaptation, Maximum Transition, and Maximum Strength phases, either within a week or within a single session of training.

Whether this method works as a year-long training model for endurance athletes is still unclear, and for that reason I would not recommend it for road cyclists. Weight lifters using this model have shown greater improvements in strength performance than weight lifters following the linear model, but researchers do not yet know what is going on at the cellular level and cannot yet pinpoint the physiological reason for the advantage.

FIGURE 10: Reverse Linear Periodization

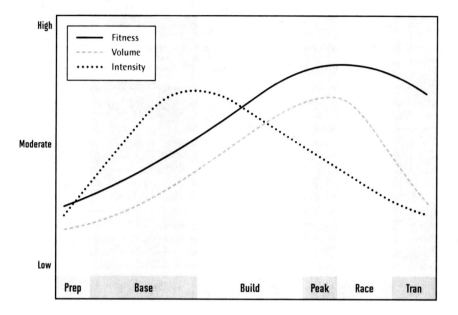

Reverse Linear Periodization

Figure 10 shows the reverse of the classic periodization model shown in Figure 8. In reverse linear periodization training, intensity is high in the Base period, whereas volume increases most significantly in the Build period. This model works best for athletes training for long, steady events such as century or even double-century rides. High-intensity workouts are incorporated with otherwise low-volume training early in the season to boost aerobic capacity (VO_2max). These high-intensity workouts are typically focused on two- to four-minute intervals done at CP6 power or heart rate zone 5b with equal time for recovery. Later in the season, lower-intensity, longer workouts develop aerobic endurance. This method can therefore bring you into excellent fitness for particularly long events, but it is not as effective for shorter, faster races.

The periodization platform you choose should be one that you understand and are committed to. Linear periodization is generally the easiest model to understand and put into place, and it is still the model used by most athletes around the world, regardless of their levels of performance. The other models have very little established research behind them, and training guidelines are therefore lacking. Trying to create and follow such a plan would involve a lot of trial and error and would likely result in uneven performances. Most athletes are well-advised to use the linear periodization model to establish general fitness in the Base period and specific fitness in the Build period. With linear periodization, you will know you are following a well-researched, proven plan for success.

8: The Training Year

You may recall from *The Cyclist's Training Bible* that there are several steps to be followed in creating your annual training plan. They are:

1. Determine your season goals
2. Establish your training objectives
3. Set your annual training hours
4. Prioritize the races you plan to do
5. Divide your year into periods
6. Assign your weekly hours

CYCLIST'S
TRAINING BIBLE
3rd ed.

See pp. 102–114 for more on the Annual Training Plan

Planning your season and actually following the plan are two entirely separate things. There are a number of pitfalls awaiting you once you have a plan in hand and start to train. Let's examine them.

CHANGING THE ANNUAL TRAINING PLAN

Once you have created an Annual Training Plan, there are two blunders you must avoid. The first is the more common—ignoring the plan and simply training as you always have. I hope that once you've put in the time to create a solid plan, one that will help produce your best race results ever, you won't disregard it. That would be a considerable waste of both your planning time and your training time. The second mistake is the opposite—to pay *too much* attention to the plan and not make changes when dictated by new circumstances. I'm not talking about circumstances like wanting to go on the group ride on a scheduled rest day. I mean those times when you realize that you are making inadequate progress, or you begin missing workouts because something unexpected has happened. Be realistic in these situations and adapt the plan as needed.

Inadequate Progress

When you're not making the progress you had expected, you must make strategic changes in your plan. You'll know whether you're making progress because you will perform a test and compare the results with the training objectives you have established. The test could be a field test, a test done in a clinic, or a C-priority race. Figure 11 shows how to handle the results. Basically, you will compare them with your planned objectives and see if you are on track or not quite up to par. If your progress is good, you will continue following the plan. If you're not happy with your progress, you must reevaluate the plan and decide what must change.

FIGURE 11: Planning, Implementation, and Analysis Model

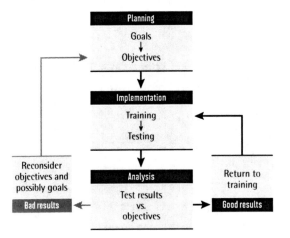

What could need changing? It could be that you didn't spend enough time in the Base period and some of your basic abilities are lacking. This is the most common mistake athletes make—they can't wait to get to the hard training of the Build period, so they cut the Base period short. The solution is simply to go back to Base 3 for a few weeks to strengthen endurance, force, and speed skills. Of these, if you have made the Base period shorter than it should have been, poor endurance is the most likely problem.

Or it may be that your objectives, and perhaps even your goals, were set unrealistically high. This mistake is especially common in athletes in the first couple of years of bike racing. After you've had a chance to implement the plan and test your progress, it may become clear that you expected too much. Give some thought to revising your goals and objectives at this point.

Another common cause of poor progress is simply doing the wrong sort of training. The problem may be that you are spending too much time training your strengths while giving your limiters only lip service. As explained in Chapter 6 of the *Training Bible*, the focus of most of your training must be on those race-specific weaknesses—limiters—that are holding you back. The tendency among self-coached athletes is to spend more training time on what they are already good at than on their weaknesses. Realize that it is only by training your limiters that you will obtain better results.

When you're not making the progress you had expected, you must make strategic changes in your plan.

Doing too many group workouts can be a problem. If you are going along with the group, you may not be focusing on what you really need to focus on for that workout session. There are times when having training partners can be very beneficial, but group workouts are often detrimental, especially in the Base period. You may either be working too hard or too easy, depending on the skills and experience of your riding partners. Look for partners who are of similar ability, and decide on a workout before starting. Unstructured group workouts tend to become "races." In the Build period this may be beneficial, but only if done in moderation. If your objectives for the ride are compatible with those of the group, then go ahead and take advantage of the camaraderie.

Missing Workouts—or More

It happens to everyone. Your training is going well, you've been consistent, and you can tell that your fitness is progressing. Then your job throws you a curve ball and you have to miss a day or more of training. Or you catch a winter virus and don't train for four days while your body is fighting it off. Maybe your knee becomes inflamed and the doctor says no riding for two weeks, or you decide you're too tired to train and need an extra day off. What should you do? Should you try to fit in the missed workouts at a later time by wedging them in between the others? Or do you just continue on as if nothing happened? How will this affect your race preparation? Here is how to handle such dilemmas.

Missing three or fewer days. For downtime of just a few days, continue training with no adjustments. The worst thing you can do is to try to fit in the lost workouts. That will not only set you up for poor training quality due to accumulated fatigue but increase the potential for a breakdown, such as an overuse injury, an illness, or the early stages of overtraining.

Missing four to seven days. If you've missed more than a few days, some rearranging is required. You'll need to readjust your workouts for up to two weeks, but you won't be able to do all of the missed workouts plus those originally planned over that time period. You'll need to be selective. The most important workouts to retain are the ones related to your limiters. Reorganize your schedule so that you can do most of those, although that may mean skipping some of the workouts that maintain your strengths. Be sure to include easy days just as you would normally do in training. Don't try to cram more hard training into fewer days.

Missing one to two weeks. If you miss one or two weeks of training, step back one mesocycle and omit an entire chunk of the training you had planned to do in the future, rather than trying to merge the lost workouts into your existing plan. For example, say you missed two weeks of training in Build 2. When ready to train normally again, go back to Build 1 for two weeks and do the appropriate workouts. Adjust your plan by cutting out two weeks of training that were scheduled to take place later in the season. One way to do this is to make Build 2 three weeks long instead of four and omit Peak 1.

Missing more than two weeks. Missing a significant block of time, such as two weeks or more, requires a return to the Base period, as one or more of the basic abilities—endurance, force, or speed skills—has probably been compromised. If you were already in the Base period when the training time was lost, step back one mesocycle. Let's say you were in Base 3 and had to miss three weeks of training for some reason. Return to Base 2. If you were in Build 2 when it happened, go back to Base 3 and then continue on from this new starting point. You will need to make major revisions to your Annual Training Plan to accommodate this change by omitting some portion of Build 2 and by possibly shortening the Peak period from two weeks to one.

No matter which of these unfortunate situations occurs, you will have less fitness on race day than you had originally hoped. You can't force in the extra workouts, because there is a limit to how much stress your body can handle. You can't force it to become just as fit on less training. This is why it is so important to avoid taking high risks in training; if you become injured, you could miss critical training hours while forced to take time off to recuperate. In any case, remember that missing some training isn't a disaster, it's simply a situation that you need to manage. Adjust your plan and move on.

NEVER COMPROMISE RECOVERY

Consistency is the key to success in athletic training. If you train inconsistently as a result of frequent physical breakdowns or mental burnout, you will never achieve a high level of race readiness. To maintain consistent training, you must provide adequate recovery days every week. One of those days should be very light. For an athlete who trains fewer than 10 hours each week, this could mean a day off; for someone who does 15 hours a week, it could mean doing an hour of weight lifting instead of riding; and for a 20-hour-per-week athlete, it could mean a two-hour, easy ride on the light day. The other weekly recovery workouts should be done at a low intensity—in heart rate zones 1 or 2.

There are two common ways to blend recovery days and high-stress training days within a training week. For the rider who is fairly new to the sport or who recovers slowly, alternating hard and easy days generally works best, as in the following example:

Monday	Day off
Tuesday	Long or intense ride
Wednesday	Short, very low-intensity ride
Thursday	Long or intense ride
Friday	Short, very low-intensity ride
Saturday	Long, high-intensity ride
Sunday	Long, low-intensity ride

An experienced rider, or one who recovers very quickly, might see better results from grouping high-stress workouts on back-to-back days and having an easy day for recovery:

Monday	Day off or light training
Tuesday	Long or intense ride
Wednesday	Long or intense ride
Thursday	Long or intense ride
Friday	Short, very low-intensity ride
Saturday	Long, high-intensity ride
Sunday	Long, low-intensity ride

We'll look at recovery in training more closely in *Companion* Chapter 18, and Chapter 9 will explore the timing of your workouts.

Not everyone respects recovery days. I often see self-coached athletes miss workouts or become frustrated with their progress, then overcompensate by making their recovery days harder. That's exactly the wrong thing to do. You will only create more fatigue and lower your workout quality on the harder days. The solution in this case is to make the hard training days harder and the easy days easier. Making workouts harder means either making them longer, doing them at a higher intensity, or doing more high-intensity volume, such as more intervals. Whatever your approach, never compromise recovery to gain fitness. It doesn't work.

9: Planning Workouts

The subject of this chapter is understanding and applying the principles of workout scheduling. It will help you determine the key workouts for each week of the season and have a good understanding of how they blend into a weekly schedule.

CYCLIST'S
TRAINING BIBLE
3rd ed.

See pp. 121–130
for more on
Weekly Routines

THE TIMING OF WORKOUTS

A specified pattern of when to do particular workouts may not work for your particular lifestyle, job, facility availability, and training groups. How then do you schedule your training sessions? By taking all of the above factors into account and designing your own customized training week, one that you can repeat week after week for the entire season with only minor changes as new circumstances arise. Here's how to do that.

Anchor workouts. These are workouts that must occur on given days each week and over which you have little or no control. For example, if your team or club rides on Wednesdays and Saturdays, that's when you must plug these sessions into your weekly plan. If you lift weights and the club availability or your work schedule only allows this to occur on Mondays and Fridays, that is when these anchor workouts must be placed in your weekly plan. Your longest bike ride may also be an anchor workout, since most working people and students must do these on the weekend.

The first step in designing your customized training week is to create a sample seven-day schedule and write in your anchor workouts on the appropriate days. Use a pencil, as you may still have a little juggling to do.

A specified pattern of when to do particular workouts may not work for your particular lifestyle, job, facility availability, and training groups. Take all of these factors into account and design your own customized training week.

Time-flexible workouts. The remaining workouts may be done on other days of the week of your choice. If you are a high-training-volume athlete and do six or more workouts each week, then scheduling one of those each day will be fairly straightforward. But if you do only three or four weekly rides, spacing them becomes very important.

For example, if you ride three times each week, you would not want those rides to be on Saturday, Sunday, and Monday with no riding for the next four days. With that many days off the bike, you would lose any physical gains you made every week. Instead, separate the rides by two or three rest days. For example, perhaps you could ride on Sundays, Tuesdays, and Fridays. Once you've determined the best days for these time-flexible workouts, add them to your sample weekly schedule.

Daily order of workouts. You probably have little or no control over the time of day for your anchor workouts. But with the flexible workouts, you must schedule the time to address one important concern: You must allow for recovery so that the hard workouts are just that—hard. In designing your optimal week, arrange the high-intensity sessions, such as intervals, fast group rides, and hill work, so that you go into them with legs that are fresh and not cooked from the workout the day before.

For example, in the Base 1 period, strength training is a high priority. Those workouts should be arranged so that you are fresh for them, which means riding easily the day before a weight session. But in all the following periods, on-bike training trumps weight training. Adjust the workout days accordingly on your sample weekly schedule.

Time between workouts. If you are doing two or more workouts on the same day, it is generally best to provide for some rest and rejuvenation between them. You will reap greater benefits from your training if you are at least partially recovered from the day's first session before starting the next. The time between workouts should include refueling and is best spent sitting down whenever possible.

ONE WORKOUT OR TWO?

Instead of doing a single, three-hour ride, is it just as good to do two 90-minute rides on the same day? The answer depends on the purpose of the workout. If your purpose is to improve speed skills, force, muscular endurance, power, or anaerobic endurance, the answer is yes. In fact, in all of these cases, two rides on the same day are far preferable to a single long ride because of the built-in recovery period between rides.

If your purpose is to improve endurance for long events, however, two workouts on the same day are seldom beneficial. One long workout is better than two shorter ones in this case. Here's why. The physiological benefits of endurance workouts require that you stress not only the many parts of the aerobic system—primarily the heart, lungs, and blood—but also the muscular and nervous systems. In addition, energy-, hormone-, and enzyme-production improvements are necessary for aerobic fitness to increase.

For example, look at how the body produces energy from fats and carbohydrates during moderate-intensity exercise. As you start a workout, the body relies heavily on carbohydrate stores to provide energy. But as the duration of the workout increases, there is a steady shift from carbohydrate burning to fat burning. Shifting into this fat-burning condition as soon as possible is one of the benefits of aerobic exercise that improves endurance. Riding twice for 90 minutes rather than taking one three-hour ride means you will spend less time that day using fat for fuel and therefore produce a smaller benefit for the energy-production system.

One longer workout is better for stimulating this and all of the previously listed endurance functions. There is also a psychological benefit that comes from completing long workouts.

———————————

It may take a few tries, but once you've accounted for all of these factors you will have your own customized weekly plan. This plan will optimize your available time and produce the greatest race readiness possible given your lifestyle.

10: Stage Race Training

For the serious cyclist, a stage race is often the most important event of the year. It is essential not to take stage-race preparation lightly. This chapter covers training and planning for these longer, critical races.

CYCLIST'S
TRAINING BIBLE
3rd ed.

*See pp. 134–138
for more on
Planning*

THE RACE PLAN

As with any race, attaining the performance and results you want in a stage race largely depends on having an effective strategy. A race strategy is nothing more than a plan for each stage that covers the variables over which you have control. You don't, for example, have control over the weather or over the fitness level of your competition. You can, however, plan for how to respond to various weather conditions, or how to position yourself relative to other riders. If you ride for a well-managed team, your role in each stage will be well defined. Unfortunately, many teams are not so well organized.

Any plan, even a sketchy one, is better than none at all. Typically, the longer the stage, the more complex the plan. The plan for a short criterium or time trial will include only a few items, whereas a plan for a long road race will include many possible tactics to achieve team or individual goals.

The plan is most effective when written down, and I like to have athletes do this about a week before the race. If you have a coach, share your plan with him or her. If not, discuss it with another teammate to make sure it is reasonable and that you haven't overlooked something important.

Sample Race Plan

Athlete: John H.

Race: Hoosierville Stage 2 Road Race

Race Date: July 18

Start Time: 10 a.m.

Race Category: 35+

Course: Five laps on an 8-mile circuit with one 0.5-mile climb of about 6–8 percent grade, then a winding descent. The climb is about 1.5 miles from the finish. Overall, a rolling course with four corners and not many wind breaks. The course favors my strengths.

Expected Weather: Hot with temps in high 80s at start time. No rain expected. Has been windy in past.

Pre-Race Meal: My usual, which works well for me.

Race Nutrition: Sports drink only.

Warm-up: The race should start fast so I will make sure I'm ready. Warm-up will include 20 minutes on the turbo trainer, steadily lifting my power and heart rate, followed by 3 to 5 jumps on a short hill near the start.

Start Position: The road is narrow at the start so I want to be in the first or second row. There will probably be about 50 riders total.

Race Goal: Win the stage (primary goal). Finish in the top 3 (secondary goal).

Last Year's Results: 5th.

How the Race Played Out Last Year: There were several attempts to establish breaks early on, but none of them worked until Tom R. got away with Ralph H. on the climb with a little over a lap to go. They worked well together. Before we organized a chase, Bill P. took off alone. We closed the gap and almost caught Bill at the line. I was second in the sprint to Tom R.

Expected Competition: Three of the top four from last year. Tom R., who won last time, has a team that isn't as strong this year. I expect him to make a move to get away early, probably on the climb. Bill P., the National TT Champ, usually tries to solo late in the race. He has no team to support him. Ralph H. will sit in all day hoping for a sprint. He will use his team to pull back breaks and set him up for the finish. No one else is really a strong contender, and I don't expect the other teams to be active either.

Sample Race Plan, continued

Strategy: Roger, Jim, and I will stay near the front of the peloton. We will watch for moves from Tom, Bill, and Ralph. Roger and Jim will help other teams chase down any breaks early on. I will go with any moves made by Tom, Bill, or Ralph and try to minimize how much work I do, saving something for the finishing sprint. I expect these moves to come on the 4th or 5th lap on the hill or after the second corner, when we are likely to hit a guttering crosswind. I'll be near the front and on the left side of the group as we approach each of these points.

The race plan takes shape during the previous twelve weeks as you're preparing for the stage race. One week before the race, you should have a pretty good idea of what you are capable of doing in the various stages. Start with your season's goal for this A-priority event. Does it still seem reasonable? Has your training gone as expected? If so, it should be easy to prepare the plan. If not, consider what you are capable of doing—either at a higher or lower level than originally thought—and create a plan that addresses the revised goal.

Of course, there could be more than one race goal, with some goals more important than others. There is no limit on secondary goals. For example, you might have a secondary goal of helping a teammate win a stage, of completing a time trial in a given time, or of simply building a higher level of fitness to boost your race performances in the following weeks.

Consider yourself a student of bike racing. When you attend races as a spectator or watch them on television, pay close attention to what is happening. Notice how the various teams' tactics play out. Bike racing is like playing chess on wheels. Understanding what your opponent is trying to accomplish will improve your defense while allowing you opportunities to have a better offense. A good resource for helping you grow as a tactical rider is Thomas Prehn's book *Racing Tactics for Cyclists* (VeloPress 2003).

Tactics are important because the outcomes of road races are usually determined by 2- to 4-minute episodes that create a separation of riders. The most common of these occur on hills, in crosswinds, and in the lead-out to the finish line for a sprint. If you improve your anaerobic endurance, you'll be physically ready for these critical moments. Having the tactical

CYCLIST'S
TRAINING BIBLE
3rd ed.

*See pp. 82–84 for
more on Training
of Abilities*

savvy to position yourself correctly is an altogether different matter, however. Physical fitness can easily be established by training alone, following the guidelines in Chapter 6 of the *Training Bible* and the sample workouts in Appendix C. But to become adept at proper positioning for hills, wind, and sprints, you need to ride with a group. This is the primary reason to train with others.

Most riders who engage in group training do so without any purpose other than to "get in a hard workout." Group rides become more useful, however, if you take time to consider the types of tactical situations you need to master in order to improve your race performance. There are several common positioning mistakes that riders make: becoming boxed in on the right-hand side of the road when approaching a hill, ending up too far back in the peloton when coming into a crosswind section, and being on the front on an approach to a sprint finish, for example. Group rides are excellent opportunities to improve your tactical skills in such situations.

Of course, stage races are not just made up of road races, although they play a big role in the General Classification. Criteriums seldom have much impact on the GC. Finishing the race with the main field will generally maintain a GC contender's ranking. Time trials, however, are another story. In many stage races, especially those with flat road-race courses, the time trial is the chief determiner of the final GC. Getting on your time trial bike once a week for the last eight weeks leading up to the race and doing a muscular-endurance workout will do wonders for your stage-race preparation and final ranking.

CYCLIST'S
TRAINING BIBLE
3rd ed.

*See pp. 257–258
for examples
of Muscular-
Endurance
Workouts*

11: Case Studies

You may recall that in *The Cyclist's Training Bible* we considered the profiles of four very different athletes to explore how different the annual training plan can be from one athlete to the next. In each instance there were factors that informed the approach to training, sometimes altering the length of time needed for a particular period or shifting the emphasis in training to address specific limiters or time restrictions. Now we are going to take the process one step further and look at how that annual training plan plays out in a few key weeks.

In some cases we'll be looking at deviations from the athletes' original Annual Training Plans (see Chapter 11 of the *Training Bible*). As we found in *Companion* Chapters 8 and 9, knowing how to adapt your plan over the course of the season will make your training even more effective.

I've included two new case studies at the end of this chapter to help athletes who are new to training with power or are finding that aging requires a new approach to training.

SINGLE-PEAK SEASON

Profile Recap

Tom Brown, age 39, is in his third year of racing. His Annual Training Plan is proof of his commitment to training and consistency this year, which will improve his greatest cycling limiter—endurance. Testing revealed that Tom has the ability to achieve his goals, though he lacks confidence. He plans to work on his mental skills. While his maximum power tested high, his power at lactate threshold is relatively low. He is also limited by low muscular endurance, a major weakness when it comes to road racing.

**CYCLIST'S
TRAINING BIBLE
3rd ed.**

*See pp. 139–141
for Tom's Annual
Training Plan*

Sample Weeks

In the Base period, Tom's training emphasizes aerobic endurance with a gradual increase in muscular endurance work. He also needs to work on cornering, so his training throughout the Base period includes many skill-development sessions. Table 2 shows his daily training schedule for weeks 19 and 22 of his Annual Training Plan. I've selected these two weeks because they provide a good example of how training can change from Base 3 to Build 1. Note the increase in the intensity of his workouts from Base 3 to Build 1 (Table 2). I also chose these two weeks because they represent some of Tom's highest-volume training, since they come shortly before his early-season races and important fitness tests.

TABLE 2: Tom Brown, Weeks 19 and 22

	DAY	TRAINING SESSION (see Appendix C for details)	DURATION (hrs:min)
Week 19 (Base 3)	Mon.	Weights: Strength Maintenance (SM)	1:00
	Tue.	Muscular Endurance: Tempo (M1)	1:30
	Wed.	Speed Skills: Cornering (S3)	1:00
	Thur.	Endurance/Force/Speed Skills: Fixed Gear (E3)	1:30
	Fri.	Endurance: Recovery (E1) or day off	1:00
	Sat.	Endurance: Aerobic (E2)	2:30
	Sun.	Endurance: Recovery (E1)	2:00
Week 22 (Build 1)	Mon.	Weights: Strength Maintenance (SM)	1:00
	Tue.	Muscular Endurance: Hill Cruise Intervals (M3)	1:00
	Wed.	Speed Skills: Cornering (S3)	1:00
	Thur.	Force: Long Hills (F2)	1:30
	Fri.	Day off	0:00
	Sat.	Muscular Endurance: Hill Cruise Intervals (M3)	2:00
	Sun.	Endurance: Aerobic (E2)	2:30

LOTS OF TIME AND LIMITERS

Profile Recap

Lisa Harvey, age 27, is a Category II cyclist who has been racing for four years. In the past her training was free-form, so many of her basic abilities are weak. She has good power, owing primarily to her ability to turn the cranks at high cadence. She has always been a good sprinter. Her limiters are force, climbing, and muscular endurance. While her endurance is not as bad as the other limiters, she nevertheless needs to improve it.

Lisa has faced frequent illness in the past two years, so in spite of her accommodating schedule, she will be looking to improve her recovery practices and carefully evaluate how she is handling training volume.

Sample Weeks

Table 3 shows Lisa's training for weeks 32 and 33 when she has races scheduled. The C-priority criterium race in week 32 is short, 45 minutes, but with warm-up and cool-down she will ride about 90 minutes that day. Nothing is changed about her normal Build 2 training routine for this week, since the race is a low priority and being treated as a hard workout. Note that this does not mean she won't give it her best effort. It would be a mistake to go into any race with the idea of holding back. Lisa realizes, however, that since she hasn't rested before this race, her results are likely to be subpar.

CYCLIST'S
TRAINING BIBLE
3rd ed.

See pp. 142–144 for Lisa's Annual Training Plan

The following weekend she will have a B-priority, 30 km time trial on Sunday. As it comes at the end of a recovery week, Lisa should feel rested and ready for a hard effort and might expect good results, even though the time trial is not her specialty. Notice that while Lisa's Annual Training Plan called for 5 hours and 30 minutes (5:30) of total training time this week, she has scheduled 6:30 instead. You must not be a slave to the volume numbers in your Annual Training Plan. They are there as general guidelines only. To train only 5:30 in week 33 would have required her to take another day off, with a resulting drop in fitness. Given the lower-than-normal intensity of the early part of this week and the already shortened training hours, she should recover nicely and be ready to race well on the weekend.

TABLE 3: Lisa Harvey, Weeks 32 and 33

	DAY	TRAINING SESSION (see Appendix C for details)	DURATION (hrs:min)
Week 32 (Build 2)	Mon.	Weights: Strength Maintenance (SM)	1:00
	Tue.	Muscular Endurance Force: Hill Cruise Intervals (M3)	1:30
	Wed.	Endurance: Aerobic (E2) on TT bike	1:00
	Thur.	Force: Moderate Hills (F1)	1:00
	Fri.	Endurance: Recovery (E1) or day off	1:00
	Sat.	Race: Falcon Field Crit (C priority)	1:30
	Sun.	Endurance: Recovery (E1)	2:30
Week 33 (Build 2)	Mon.	Weights: Strength Maintenance (SM), easy on legs	1:00
	Tue.	Speed Skills: Sprints (S6)	1:00
	Wed.	Endurance: Aerobic (E2) on TT bike	1:00
	Thur.	Speed Skills: Form Sprints (S5)	1:00
	Fri.	Day off	0:00
	Sat.	Endurance: Aerobic (E2) on TT bike. Include a few race efforts of 90 sec.	1:00
	Sun.	Race: Road to Nowhere TT (B priority)	1:30

THREE RACE PEAKS

Profile Recap

Sam Crooks, age 37, has raced in both Category III and masters races for four years. He fits in workouts around his busy schedule as he can. Maximum power and speed skills are Sam's strong points, making him an excellent criterium racer; but his marginal endurance, climbing, and muscular endurance limit his performance in road races and time trials.

Sample Weeks

CYCLIST'S TRAINING BIBLE 3rd ed.

See pp. 144–146 for Sam's Annual Training Plan

Here is a great example of how to schedule two race weeks. Table 4 includes Sam Crooks's first race of the season, which appears on the schedule during his highest-volume week of the year—Base 3, week 8. Getting in about 15 hours this week will be a challenge for Sam, given his work schedule. There are two rides scheduled for Wednesday that week. The first will likely be done indoors on a trainer before work, since in February it will be dark in

TABLE 4: Sam Crooks, Weeks 8 and 30

	DAY	TRAINING SESSION (see Appendix C for details)	DURATION (hrs:min)
Week 8 (Base 3)	Mon.	Weights: Strength Maintenance (SM)	1:00
	Tue.	Endurance: Aerobic (E2)	1:30
	Wed.	A.M.–Endurance: Aerobic (E2)	1:00
		P.M.–Force: Long Hills (F2)	1:30
	Thur.	Endurance: Recovery (E1)	1:30
	Fri.	Speed Skills: Form Sprints (S5)	1:30
	Sat.	Race: Crossville RR (C priority). Ride for 1 hr. after race (E1).	3:30
	Sun.	Endurance: Aerobic (E2)	3:30
Week 30 (Race)	Mon.	Day off	0:00
	Tue.	Anaerobic Endurance: 5 x 90 sec. @ CP6 (3 min. recoveries). Otherwise ride aerobic (E2).	2:00
	Wed.	Anaerobic Endurance: 4 x 90 sec. @ CP6 (3 min. recoveries). Otherwise ride aerobic (E2).	1:30
	Thur.	Anaerobic Endurance: 3 x 90 sec. @ CP6 (3 min. recoveries). Otherwise ride recovery (E1).	1:00
	Fri.	Day off	0:00
	Sat.	Power: 1 set of 5 Jumps (P1)	1:00
	Sun.	Race: Greenville RR (A priority)	2:30

the morning. The second Wednesday ride will be immediately after work, and since the sun goes down early he may need to start this ride from his office to get it in before dark. After Saturday's C-priority race, Sam will ride for an hour to cool down. And with a long ride on Sunday, Sam will be able to complete his biggest week in years. As he will have built up to this high-volume week over a period of several months, his endurance should be at an all-time high by week's end. Following a recovery week, he should be ready to start into the Build period with much lower volume but more intensity.

Of course, all of his plans for a high-volume week could be for naught should this wind up being a week that he has his children visiting. As with most riders, there are many complications in trying to create the perfect training plan, and you must be willing to be flexible.

Table 4 also details Week 30, one of Sam's lowest-volume weeks of the season, culminating with an A-priority race on Sunday. The emphasis this week will be on maintaining anaerobic endurance by doing intervals at his aerobic-capacity power (CP6). Notice that the number of intervals decreases during the week, and that there are relatively long recoveries after each interval to prevent excessive fatigue. The day off on Friday will help ensure that he is rested going into the weekend. It is better to take the day off, or do a very easy ride, two days before the race rather than the day before. After a day of complete rest the day before a race, riders often complain of being "flat" on race day. Some high-intensity work on Saturday should prevent this.

SUMMER BASE TRAINING

Profile Recap

Randy Stickler, age 25, is a college student who has been racing over ten years. He has been on the national team as a Category I cyclist in several high-profile races both nationally and internationally. Because he carries a full load of classes, his weekends are dedicated to training. His greatest abilities are endurance, force, muscular endurance, power, and climbing. Randy's short sprint is excellent, but his longer sprints fade in races. Consequently, he considers anaerobic endurance to be a limiter.

CYCLIST'S
TRAINING BIBLE
3rd ed.

*See pp. 146–148
for Randy's Annual
Training Plan*

Sample Weeks

In week 21, as illustrated in Table 5, Randy will be starting to peak for an A-priority race—the Colorado State Road Championships. For him, the 17 weekly hours will be moderate as he begins tapering. The following week, volume will drop to just over 13 hours, with about 11 hours the week of State Roads. During these three weeks the emphasis will be on well-spaced, high intensity training. Notice that in week 21 he will have only two hard training days—Wednesday and Sunday. The Sunday race is a B-priority, so his training will be relatively light for the three preceding days. The group ride on Wednesday should last about 90 minutes and is expected to be quite intense, as most of the top riders in the area show up for this workout in the early summer months. To make that ride even more like State Roads, he will do hill intervals before the group ride. This workout should leave him quite fatigued, so two of the next three days are short recovery rides.

The Sunday road race is in the mountains, so there will be considerable climbing. After the race, a point-to-point event, he will ride back to the start

TABLE 5: Randy Stickler, Weeks 21 and 28

	DAY	TRAINING SESSION (see Appendix C for details)	DURATION (hrs:min)
Week 21 (Peak)	Mon.	Weights: Strength Maintenance (SM)	1:00
	Tue.	Endurance: Aerobic (E2)	2:30
	Wed.	Anaerobic Endurance: Hill Intervals (A4) before Group Ride (A1)	3:30
	Thur.	Endurance: Recovery (E1)	2:00
	Fri.	Endurance: Aerobic (E2). Within this ride do 4–6 Hill Sprints (P2).	2:00
	Sat.	Endurance: Recovery (E1)	2:00
	Sun.	Race: Ironhorse RR (B priority). Long cool-down after race.	4:00
Week 28 (Base 3)	Mon.	Weights: Strength Maintenance (SM), easy on legs	1:00
	Tue.	Endurance: Aerobic (E2)	3:30
	Wed.	Muscular Endurance: Group Ride (A1). Sit in. Long warm-up and cool-down.	4:00
	Thur.	Endurance: Recovery (E1)	2:30
	Fri.	Speed Skills: Form Sprints (S5)	2:00
	Sat.	Race: Crit. (C priority). Long warm-up and cool-down.	3:30
	Sun.	Race: Grand Junction RR (C priority). Long cool-down.	5:00

area to log even more climbing. This will help prepare him for the Mount Evans Hill Climb, which is two weeks after State Roads.

Week 28 is the second of a four-week Base period. It will include increased volume to reestablish Randy's endurance after eight weeks of reduced-duration training while he prepares for two A-priority races. This week will end with two races, but his volume will not be compromised because they are C-priorities. With four rides of more than three hours each that week, he should make significant gains in aerobic endurance. Notice the instructions for Wednesday's group ride to "sit in." After eight weeks of high-intensity work, Randy doesn't need to further develop his power capabilities or anaerobic endurance. The plan shifts instead to increased endurance, and intensity must drop accordingly so that he can avoid injury or burnout later in the season.

Following three weeks of increased volume, Randy's aerobic endurance should be well established. That will allow him to emphasize intensity once again in preparation for his last A-priority race of the season. But if his aerobic endurance isn't sufficient, he will do more Base training starting in week 31 and continue until it is at the optimal level. See "Measuring Intensity with Power" in *Companion* Chapter 4 for a discussion of how to determine this.

CASE STUDY: NEW TO TRAINING WITH POWER

Profile

Marlene Ziehl is a 39-year-old who has been competitive in her race category for the past five years. She started racing at age 32 and rapidly developed the fitness to become a contender at races throughout Arizona where she lives. Since she moves up to a new age category this season, she would like to test herself at a higher level by racing Masters Nationals for the first time. Her focus will be on the time trial, which is her strongest event. This will require raising all of her fitness abilities, but especially force and muscular endurance, to higher levels.

She is a physical therapist with 10-hour workdays on Mondays, Wednesdays, and Fridays. Time for workouts is quite limited on these days. She can get in the bulk of her training on Tuesdays and Thursdays, when she works half-days, as well as on weekends, when she is off from work.

Plan

Marlene purchased a power meter right at the start of this season and is learning how to use it. One of the first things she did was a CP30 test to establish her training zones. A 30-minute time trial done as a workout serves as an approximation of CP60. She could have raced a time trial of about 40 km to establish her CP60, but no such race was available in November when she got the power meter. A 60-minute race is always preferable to a field test for establishing zones, since you go harder when racing than when training.

A 30-minute test done as a solo workout is a good substitute for a 60-minute test done during a race because it typically produces similar results in terms óf power output. Think about it this way: If you were to ride a 20 km workout solo, or race in a 20 km event with several hundred competitors, which one would give you the faster time? The race, of course, because of the added motivation. In fact, your 20 km workout pace would be about equal to a 40 km race pace. That's because you ride about 5 percent faster in a race than in a workout of the same distance. So a 30-minute time trial as a workout will predict fairly accurately the power, pace, and speed you would achieve in a 60-minute race.

Marlene's CP30 test predicted her CP60 to be 210 watts, establishing her zones as shown in Table 6.

TABLE 6: Marlene Ziehl's Power Training Zones (watts)

ZONE 1	ZONE 2	ZONE 3	ZONE 4	ZONE 5	ZONE 6	ZONE 7
Recovery	Aerobic	Tempo	Threshold	Aerobic capacity	Anaerobic capacity	Power
<118	118–158	159–189	190–220	221–252	253–315	>315

Note: See Chapter 4 for details of how to establish power training zones.

To accomplish her first season goal of winning the State Time Trial Championship (see Figure 12), Marlene would need to raise her CP60 from 210 watts to at least 220. With a current body weight of 125 pounds (57 kg) and a CP60 of 210 watts, she produces about 3.7 watts per kilogram. She is already competitive in the time trial at the state level, and the extra 10 watts is a reasonable gain to expect by April 20 (as per her Training Objectives on the Annual Training Plan). Ultimately, she will need to be at 4 watts per kilogram at CP60 to achieve her second season goal of becoming a top-ten contender at nationals. That means lifting her CP60 by at least 10 percent in eight months of training. This will not be easy, but it is realistic, given her profile.

Marlene will start in the weight room by focusing on building greater force. She will work to elevate her squat to 160 pounds (about 1.3 times her body weight) from a starting point of about 140 pounds—a 14 percent increase, which is reasonable to expect in this amount of time. That should be accomplished by the middle of January. At that point her training will shift toward developing greater bike-specific force with big gear intervals and, later, hill repeats done at zone 3 and, eventually, zone 4 power.

For her third goal of finishing with the field in the Masters Nationals, her greatest limiter is anaerobic endurance. Although this goal is not quite

FIGURE 12: Sample Annual Training Plan (New to Training with Power)

Athlete: *Marlene Ziehl*   Annual hours: *700*

Seasonal goals:
1. *Win AZ State TT (sub-65 min 40 km)*
2. *Top 10 at Nats TT (sub-63 min 40 km)*
3. *Finish with field at Masters Nats RR*

Training objectives:
1. *Refine RR strategy abilities by 7/20.*
2. *Squat 1.3 x body weight by 1/27 and 6/15.*
3. *Raise CP60 to 220 w by 4/20.*
4. *Raise CP60 to 230 w by 7/6.*
5. *Raise CP6 to 255 w by 7/6.*

Wk#	Mon	Race	PRI	Period	Hours	Details	Weights	Endurance	Force	Speed Skills	Muscular Endur.	Anaerobic Endur.	Power	Testing
01	11/5			Tran										
02	11/12			Prep	12:00		AA	X		X				
03	11/19				12:00		▼	X		X				
04	11/26				12:00	*VO₂ Test	MT	X		X				*
05	12/3			Base 1	14:00		▼	X	X	X				
06	12/10				16:50		MS	X	X	X				
07	12/17				18:50			X	X	X				
08	12/24			▼	10:00			X		X				
09	12/31			Base 2	14:50			X	X	X	X			
10	1/7				17:50		▼	X	X	X	X			
11	1/14				19:50		SM	X	X	X	X			
12	1/21	Florence 20 km TT	C	▼	10:00	*Race		X		X				*
13	1/28			Base 3	15:50			X	X	X	X		X	
14	2/4	Bartlett Lake HC	C		18:50	*Race		X	•	X	•		X	
15	2/11	McDowell RR	C		20:50	*Race		X	X	X	•	•	X	
16	2/18	Florence 20 km TT	C	▼	10:00	*Race, **VO₂ Test		X		X	•		X	**
17	2/25			Build 1	17:50			X	X		X	X	X	
18	3/3	Hungry Dog Crit.	C		17:50	*Race		X	X		X	•	•	
19	3/10	Tumacacori RR	B		14:50	*Race		X	X		X	•	•	
20	3/17			▼	10:00	*CP6-30 Field Tests		X		X				*
21	3/24			Build 2	16:50			X			X	X	X	
22	3/31	Superior RR	B		13:50	*Race		X			X	•	X	
23	4/7				16:50			X			X	X	X	
24	4/14			▼	10:00	*CP6-30 Field Tests		X		X			X	*
25	4/21			Peak	14:50			X			X	X	X	
26	4/28				11:50		▼	X			X	X	X	
27	5/5	AZ State 40 km TT Champ	A	Race	10:00	*Race		X		•				
28	5/12			Build 1	17:50	*VO₂ Test (assess Base)	MT	X		X	X	X		*
29	5/19	Tucson Crit.	C		17:50		▼	X		X	X	X		
30	5/26	Tucson 20 km TT	B		14:50		MS	X		X	X	X		
31	6/2			▼	10:00	*CP6-30 Field Tests		X		X			X	
32	6/9	Tucson Crit.	C	Build 2	16:50	*Race	▼	X		X	•	•	
33	6/16	Tucson 20 km TT	B		13:50	*Race	SM	X		•	X	X	
34	6/23				16:50			X		X	X	X	
35	6/30	Tucson RR	B	▼	10:00	*CP6-30 Field Tests		X	X		•	X	*
36	7/7	Tucson 20 km TT	B	Peak	13:50			X		X	X	X	
37	7/14				11:50		▼	X		X	X	X	
38	7/21	Masters Nats	A	Race	10:00	*Race		•		X	•	•	*
39	7/28			Tran										
40	8/4													
41	8/11	Eagle Vail Century	C			*Century		•	•				
42	8/18													
43	8/25	Copper Triangle Century	C	▼		*Century		•	•				

as challenging as the two time trial goals, road racing requires a high level of anaerobic endurance. To ride strongly there she will want to raise her CP6 from 4.5 watts per kilogram (255 watts) to 4.8 (275 watts). CP6 is a good predictor of aerobic capacity, which is improved by training at zone 5 power (see Table 6). In the Build periods she will devote one or two days each week to zone 5 training to lift her CP6.

We will field-test Marlene's CP6 and CP30 frequently throughout the season to gauge her progress. At the start of the Base and Build periods, she will also undergo lab testing to determine her aerobic capacity (VO_2max), pedaling economy, and metabolic efficiency. The lab technician will help her interpret the data and understand its implications for her training.

Table 7 shows the plan for Marlene's first Build period of the season. By this time she should have a well-established base of fitness, meaning that her aerobic endurance, force, and speed skills are progressing well. Her muscular endurance should also be coming along. In this sample week she will focus on beginning to raise her muscular endurance to the level necessary to set a personal best for a 40 km time trial. The Tuesday interval workout will be done in the time trial position, but on hills to develop force while also boosting muscular endurance power. Essentially, the purpose is to improve her capacity to drive a bigger gear. Time trialing is all about who can turn the biggest gear the fastest—in other words: power. This is a workout she will do repeatedly in the Build period. The workout is conducted at CP30 power, which should rise over the course of several weeks. So the targeted power for this session will also change every few weeks.

On Sunday her long ride will be done on a hilly course on her road bike. She will stay seated on the climbs to boost her hip extension power while maintaining endurance. For further time trial preparation she will perform Friday's recovery ride on her time trial bike in the aero position. Riding the time trial bike once each week is not sufficient when preparing for an important race against the clock. The extra day each week on this bike will allow her to continue to tweak her position and become comfortable with it.

In week 17, with the workouts on Thursday and Saturday, Marlene will also be working on building her anaerobic endurance and sprint power. The Saturday group ride should be done with preliminary Masters Nationals road-race strategy and tactics in mind. The purpose of this ride is not merely fitness but also mental preparation. Over the next few weeks, the strategy

TABLE 7: Marlene Ziehl, Weeks 17 and 20

	DAY	TRAINING SESSION (see Appendix C for details)	DURATION (hrs:min)
Week 17 (Build 1)	Mon.	Weights: Strength Maintenance (SM)	1:00
	Tue.	Muscular Endurance: 5 x 6 min. Hill Cruise Intervals (M3) + 20 min. Threshold (M6), all on TT bike in aero position	3:00
	Wed.	Endurance: Recovery (E1)	1:30
	Thur.	Anaerobic Endurance + Power: Jumps (P1) + 5 x 3 min. SE Intervals (A2) + Hill Sprints (P2)	3:00
	Fri.	Endurance: Recovery (E1) on TT bike in aero position	1:30
	Sat.	Anaerobic Endurance: Group Ride (A1) focusing on elements of proposed Nats RR strategy and tactics	3:30
	Sun.	Endurance + Force: Long ride on a course with Moderate Hills (F1). Stay seated on climbs to build/maintain force.	4:00
Week 20 (Build 1)	Mon.	Weights: Strength Maintenance (SM)	1:00
	Tue.	Endurance: Recovery (E1)	3:30
	Wed.	Endurance: Recovery (E1). Optional ride based on how you feel.	1:00
	Thur.	Endurance: Aerobic (E2)	1:00
	Fri.	Test: 6 min. TT on flat course to establish CP6 on road bike	1:30
	Sat.	Test: 30 min. TT on flat course to establish CP30 on TT bike	2:00
	Sun.	Endurance + Force: Long ride on a course with Moderate Hills (F1). Stay seated on climbs to build/maintain force.	2:30

she intends to use at nationals should take shape based on what she discovers works best for her in group rides.

Week 20 from Marlene's Annual Training Plan is also shown in Table 7. This is a "rest and test" week. From experience she knows that it takes her about four consecutive days of rest to recover following a block of hard training. By Friday of that week she should be feeling rejuvenated and ready to go again. She will warm up well and then do a 6-minute time trial. On Saturday she will do a 30-minute time trial following her warm-up. Trying to do both on the same day is not a good idea for most athletes, as fatigue or low motivation is likely to affect the second test of the day. On Sunday she will do a long ride on a hilly course as usual, except this week it will be somewhat shorter.

CASE STUDY: THE AGING ATHLETE

Profile

Ralph Hearth is 56 and owns a successful business that takes a considerable amount of his time. He works around 50 hours weekly. His wife is supportive of his training and racing. He has two daughters who are away in college. Previously he raced both as a triathlete and as a road cyclist, with moderate success in both sports. With nagging running injuries, he has decided to focus on cycling this season to see what he can accomplish. There is a high likelihood that his bike fitness will bloom as a result of focused training.

Plan

Let's take a close look at Ralph's Annual Training Plan as shown in Figure 13. His "annual hours" are based not only on what he has done in the past two seasons, but also on how much time he has available for training given the many demands on his time. I normally recommend that masters athletes don't train more than 500 hours a year. By using Table 8.5 from the *Training Bible*, he sees that his highest-volume week for a 500-hour year is 15 hours. The breakdown of workouts for that week can be found in Table 9.1 from the *Training Bible*. Admittedly, Ralph knows that he may not be able to achieve all of those hours. But missing a few hours in the peak volume week is better than reducing his total annual hours. With a 500-hour seasonal volume, most of his weeks will be in the range of 10 to 13 hours, which will fit well with his lifestyle.

CYCLIST'S
TRAINING BIBLE
3rd ed.

See pp. 112–113 for Table 8.5; pp. 129–130 for Table 9.1

Now let's examine his goals. It is not generally a good idea to set a goal of finishing in the top three in a race, as there are factors affecting that result that are outside an athlete's control. The exception, however, is when you know who to expect on the starting line with you and how well prepared they are likely to be. Ralph has raced both of his A-priority events, the Wisconsin and Minnesota state road championships, many times and has seen the same riders contend for the podium spots. So he has a good idea of what to expect. He has no other goals for the season beyond winning these two races. That keeps the season and his training very simple. There is no doubt about what he needs to accomplish to have a successful year.

Ralph's training objectives (Figure 13) fall into two categories, those related to power output and those having to do with race strategy. The goals relating to power illustrate how a power meter can simplify the planning and training process. The power meter takes much of the guesswork out of knowing what you need to accomplish and allows you to gauge your progress daily against an objective measure. Used correctly, it can be the single most important piece of training equipment you can own, apart from your bike.

Ralph has determined that CP60 and CP6 power values (see Chapter 4 for more on power) are critical to his success this season. CP60 is closely related to muscular endurance, and having a high CP6 is a key to success in those brief episodes that often determine the outcome of races—making a breakaway attempt, bridging a short distance to a break that's up the road, climbing a short hill at a very high intensity, or hanging on when the group is guttered by a crosswind. CP6 is the intensity used for anaerobic endurance workouts (see Appendix C of the *Training Bible*).

Ralph's CP60 and CP6 values at the end of last season were at 230 watts and 276 watts, respectively. Based on his body weight of 158 pounds (72 kg), his CP60 is 3.2 watts per kilogram (w/kg) and his CP6 is 3.8 w/kg. To be competitive in his category for road races these need to be higher, probably at least 3.6 w/kg (260 w) and 4.2 w/kg (300 w), especially because he does not have a team to support him in races. He's done a lot of research on what his power should be relative to his weight, based on the averages for competitive male cyclists his age. Achieving these power levels by the dates listed in the Training Objectives will bring a clear focus to his training.

Ralph also needs to be better at having a race strategy and sticking to it. This has been his greatest limiter in the past. Simple race strategies are usually best. All Ralph needs to do is stay out of the wind and let others do most of the work, since he does not have a strong team to support him. He will rehearse this basic strategy in fast group rides in the Build period and in B- and C-priority races. His race tactics will evolve from the platform of this strategy.

As a 56-year-old athlete, Ralph needs to be much more concerned with his recovery than younger competitors. His periodization plan in Figure 13 reflects this. Notice that he has scheduled three-week mesocycles instead

FIGURE 13: Sample Annual Training Plan (The Aging Athlete)

Athlete: *Ralph Hearth*

Annual hours: *500*

Seasonal goals:

1. *Podium at Wisconsin State Road Championships.*
2. *Podium at Minnesota State Road Championships.*

Training objectives:

1. *Raise CP60 to 3.6+ w/kg by 4/27.*
2. *Raise CP6 to 4.2+ w/kg by 5/18.*
3. *Rebuild CP60, CP6 as above by 8/10.*
4. *Establish and refine race strategy by 6/1.*
5. *Establish and refine race strategy by 8/17.*

Wk#	Mon	Race	PRI	Period	Hours	Details	Weights	Endurance	Force	Speed Skills	Muscular Endur.	Anaerobic Endur.	Power	Testing
01	12/3			Prep	8:50		AA	X		X				
02	12/10				8:50			X		X				
03	12/17			▼	8:50	*CP6 and CP30		X		X				•
04	12/24			Base 1	10:00		MT	X	X	X				
05	12/31				12:00			X	X	X				
06	1/7			▼	7:00		MS	X		X				X
07	1/14			Base 2	10:50			X	X	X	X			
08	1/21				12:50			X	X	X	X			
09	1/28			▼	7:00	*CP30		X		X				•
10	2/4			Base 3	11:00		SM	X	X	X	X			
11	2/11				13:50			X	X	X	X			
12	2/18				7:00			X		X				X
13	2/25				13:50			X	X	X	X			
14	3/3				15:00			X	X	X	X			
15	3/10			▼	7:00	*CP6 and CP30		X		X				•
16	3/17			Build 1	12:50			X				X	X	X	
17	3/24				12:50			X				X	X	X	
18	3/31				7:00			X		X				X	X
19	4/7			Build 2	12:00			X				X	X	X	
20	4/14	Durand RR	B		10:00	*Race		X			•	•	X	
21	4/21	Woods Memorial RR	C		7:00	*Race, **CP30		X		X	•	•	X	••
22	4/28				12:00			X				X	X	X	
23	5/5				12:00			X				X	X	X	
24	5/12	Denzer RR	C	▼	7:00	*Race, **CP6		X		X	•	•	X	••
25	5/19			Peak	10:50			X				X	X	X	
26	5/26	Sussex Crit	C	▼	8:50	*Race	▼	X		X	•	•		
27	6/2	WI State Road Champs	A	Race	7:00	*Race				X	•		X	
28	6/9	WI State Crit Champs	C	Tran	9:00	3-day Tran then Base 3	MT	X	X	•	X	•	•	
29	6/16			Base 3	15:00	14 days of Base 3		X	X	X	X			
30	6/23	Brice Prairie 40 km TT	B	▼	7:00	*Race, CP60	▼	X	X	X	•			•
31	6/30	Palmyra RR	B	Build 2	10:00	*Race	SM	X			•	•	X	
32	7/7				12:00			X				X	X	X	
33	7/14				7:00	*CP30		X		X			X	•
34	7/21				12:00			X		X			X	X
35	7/28	Firehouse 50-mile TTT	B		10:00	*Race		X			•	X	X	
36	8/4			▼	7:00	*CP6 and CP30		X		X			X	•
37	8/11	Real Wheel RR	B	Peak	10:50	*Race	▼	X			•	•	X	
38	8/18	MN State Road Champs	A	Race	7:00	*Race				X	•	•	X	
39	8/25			Unstructured										
40	9/1	10 x 100 Ride	C	▼										
41	9/8	Cheq. Fat Tire 40-mile	B											
42	9/15			Tran										
43	9/22													
44	9/29													
45	10/6			▼										

of going with the more common four-week schedules, which will allow for a rest week after every two weeks of training. More frequent rest should boost the overall quality of his training. He will also carefully monitor how he is feeling and back off if he notices signs of overtraining.

Strength training is also critical for older athletes because they tend to lose muscle mass more quickly than younger athletes do. To counteract this, Ralph will continue to lift weights year round, with one session per week when following his Strength Maintenance (SM) routine.

One of the suspected causes for muscle loss in older athletes has to do with diet. As it ages, the body has a tendency toward high levels of acidity. It responds by pulling nitrogen from the muscles to prevent the acidic shift, and this causes muscle loss. Ralph will emphasize fruits and vegetables in his diet to improve his acidity balance. This strategy is explained in greater detail in Chapter 14 of the *Training Bible*.

Ralph has very few races prior to the Wisconsin State Road Championship in week 27, so he will depend heavily on group rides in the Build period to become race ready. After that, Ralph may have too many B-priority races scheduled. Since he will need to rest for three to five days before each of these, there will be some loss of fitness. The most critical one is the Firehouse 50-mile team time trial in week 35, which comes just three weeks before his second A-priority race. The B-priority race the week before the Minnesota State Road Championship is not a problem since he will be peaking with reduced volume at that time anyway.

After the Minnesota State Road Championship in mid-August, he has no more A-priority races, but there are two other events he will participate in. This will be a time of unstructured training for Ralph. He should feel free to experiment with different training methods, such as block periodization, greater intensity with much less volume, or doing more group rides to see how they affect his performance. He may well find something that works even better for him.

The key to Ralph's season is lifting his CP60 and CP6 to all-time highs. Work on this begins as soon as training starts in December, and nearly all of his training points toward these two objectives. Week 8 in Table 8 is during Ralph's Base period, when he lays the groundwork for the Build period. It is critical that he focus on Base workouts so that he later has the fitness to train with greater emphasis on muscular endurance, anaerobic endurance, and sprint power.

TABLE 8: Ralph Hearth, Weeks 8 and 28

	DAY	TRAINING SESSION (see Appendix C for details)	DURATION (hrs:min)
Week 8 (Base 2)	Mon.	Weights: Maximum Strength (MS)	1:00
	Tue.	Speed Skills: Spin-ups (S1)	1:30
	Wed.	Muscular Endurance: Tempo (M1)	1:30
	Thur.	Weights: Maximum Strength (MS)	1:00
	Fri.	Endurance: Recovery (E1)	1:30
	Sat.	Force: Moderate Hills (F1)	2:30
	Sun.	Endurance: Aerobic ride on rolling course (E2)	3:30
Week 28 (Transition)	Mon.	Weights: Maximum Transition (MT)	1:00
	Tue.	Day off	0:00
	Wed.	Day off	0:00
	Thur.	Muscular Endurance: Cruise Intervals on TT bike (M2)	2:00
	Fri.	Force: Long Hills (F2)	2:00
	Sat.	Endurance: Recovery (E1)	1:00
	Sun.	Race: State Crit. (C priority) + Endurance: Aerobic (E2)	3:00

Week 8 shows how Ralph will blend weight training with on-bike training. High power output at all durations results primarily from a cyclist having the muscular force to drive the pedal down when in a big gear. Maximum Strength (MS) training with weights, especially hip-extension exercises such as the squat, the leg press, and the step-up, builds such force. Notice that Ralph will be lifting weights twice this week, as he will have done for the previous seven weeks.

Due to the severity of Wisconsin's winters, which are characterized by limited daylight but no shortage of snow and ice, nearly all of Ralph's weekday bike training is expected to be done indoors on a trainer. To help prevent burnout from so much trainer time, the durations are held to no longer than 90 minutes. Some riders can easily manage more than that. Others find 90 minutes much too long.

The workouts Ralph has scheduled for this week are typical of Base 2. None of these bike workouts would be considered hard later in the season. But he will find these rides challenging, especially for the legs, because of the emphasis on heavy weight training in Base 2. Once strength work is cut back to Strength Maintenance (SM) in week 10, the on-bike sessions will become more challenging. The force and muscular endurance workouts will become much more intense as Base 3 starts. But he will be prepared for this as a result of the weight-room and on-bike training done in Base 2.

Week 28, also shown in Table 8, is an interesting one. This is the week following his first A-priority race of the season. The first three days will be off the bike so that Ralph can get some much-needed rest before starting back to hard training. During these three days he will assess his fitness level to determine whether he needs to reestablish his endurance, force, or speed-skills abilities. He will also factor in how well he held up in the latter stages of the previous Sunday's race, how strong he was on climbs, how he did in time trial–like situations, and how well he has been pedaling. Ralph has a tendency to slip back into a low-cadence mashing if he doesn't stay focused on pedaling smoothly. When we created his Annual Training Plan, we assumed that he would need to return to Base training at this time. As a result, we included muscular endurance, force, and endurance training in the workouts for week 28. This three-day transition period may seem challenging for a masters-level athlete, but Ralph has a high fitness level, and he will monitor his fatigue closely and back off if necessary. After three days of inactivity at this point in the season, most athletes, including masters, are anxious to get back to training.

Even though it appears in the Annual Training Plan that Ralph will only be doing one week of Base training, he actually has 14 days devoted to endurance, force, speed skills, and muscular endurance. On Thursday of week 28 he starts back into the Base period. This Base period continues through week 29 and finally ends on Wednesday of week 30. Thursday through Saturday of week 30 will be rest days to prepare for the B-priority time trial on Sunday of that week.

Notice also that Ralph is returning to Maximum Transition (MT) training in the weight room on the Monday after the time trial. He'll only do three such sessions—one each week for three weeks—and they won't be as intense as they were earlier in the year. At this point in the season, the focus of his training is on the bike. If he had twelve or more weeks until his next A-priority race, he could have gone back to Maximum Strength (MS) training with greater loads and fewer repetitions. But with such a short time to get ready for his next major event, there isn't time to recover adequately from the muscle soreness and reduced saddle time.

CYCLIST'S
TRAINING BIBLE
3rd ed.

See pp. 154–155
for more on
Strength Training
Phases

12: Strength

In *The Cyclist's Training Bible*, I outline an approach to strength training and stretching to complement your training and make your time in the gym more purposeful and effective. This regimen strengthens the muscle groups you rely on for cycling, ultimately improving your endurance and building resistance against injury. In addition to improving endurance, your strength training can also improve your speed skills and force. The exercises and programs in this chapter should help you tailor your strength training to your needs and enhance your triathlon performance considerably.

In addition to improving endurance, strength training can also improve your speed skills and force.

SEASONAL PERIODIZATION OF STRENGTH TRAINING

Strength training with weights needs to dovetail with your cycling-specific training so that the two modes are complementary. If they don't mesh well, you may find that you are frequently tired and that your bike training isn't progressing. Table 9 shows you when you should do each phase of strength training during your season.

CYCLIST'S
TRAINING BIBLE
3rd ed.

See pp. 154–157 for more on Strength Training Phases

If you have two or more Race periods in a season, I recommend that you return to the Maximum Strength (MS) phase whenever you repeat the Base period. After four to six sessions, you can return to Strength Maintenance (SM).

If your periodization plan has only one Race period, incorporate four to six MS sessions about every 16 weeks. Reduce the intensity of your

TABLE 9: Periodization of Strength Training

PERIOD	STRENGTH PHASE
Prep	AA–MT
Base 1	MS
Base 2	SM
Base 3	SM
Build 1	SM
Build 2	SM
Peak	SM
Race	(None)

cycling-specific workouts during these short MS phases, especially the day after a strength session. In essence, you are inserting mini–Base periods into your plan every 16 weeks, with an increased emphasis on strength and a decreased emphasis on bike intensity. Emphasize duration in your rides; otherwise, your bike training may decline due to the intensity of the added heavy-lifting phase.

UNDULATING PERIODIZATION OF STRENGTH TRAINING

The strength training periodization model described is called "linear" and is discussed in greater detail in *Companion* Chapter 7. That chapter also mentions that another model, "undulating" periodization, has been shown in scientific studies to be especially beneficial for the development of strength. You may find that it works better for you than linear periodization.

Using daily undulating periodization is simple. During the six weeks or so in which you would have been doing the Maximum Transition (MT) and MS phases in succession, you instead combine them into one workout. You do both MT and MS for each weight lifting exercise in each workout. If, for example, you are doing three sets, the first set is done with a load you can only lift about 15 times. The second set is with a load you can lift 10 times. And the third set is with a load you lift only 5 times.

Except for the loads, reps, and sets, the guidelines for daily undulating strength periodization match the MS phase. The sidebar shows details for this phase. During the six weeks you are using this daily undulating model, the loads should increase for each set, indicating that you are getting stronger. Of course, in the Base 1 and early Base 2 periods, on-bike workouts are low intensity with an emphasis on aerobic endurance, so this increased load

CYCLIST'S
TRAINING BIBLE
3rd ed.

*See pp. 159–165
for Strength
Exercises*

Daily Undulating Strength Phase

Total sessions/phase	12–16
Sessions/week	2–3
Load (% 1RM)	Build to nearly 90%*
Sets/session	2–3
Reps/set	Descending: 15 reps, 10 reps, 5 reps*
Speed of lift	Slow to moderate
Recovery (in minutes)	2–4*

*Only **bold** exercises listed below follow this guideline. All others continue AA guidelines.

Exercises (in order of completion):

- **Hip extension (squat, leg press, or step-up)**
- **Seated row**
- Abdominal with twist
- Upper body choice (chest press or lat pull-down)
- Personal weakness (hamstring curl, knee extension, or heel raise)
- **Standing row**

from strength training should not be an issue. The Anatomical Adaptation (AA) and SM phases are unchanged.

SUPPLEMENTAL STRENGTH TRAINING

Muscular Coordination

When we say someone has "good coordination," we mean that his or her movements have a certain smoothness and grace. "Muscular coordination" simply refers to the ability to time the contractions and relaxations of all the muscles involved in a smooth movement. For cycling, most of the body's muscles must be innervated and relaxed in an intricate pattern.

You'll notice that most of the strength exercises in Chapter 12 of the *Training Bible* involve two or more joints bending and straightening in a coordinated way. That is because single-joint exercises, such as a knee extension, do little to improve the intricate muscle-firing patterns necessary for sport performance. Multijoint exercises, such as a squat, involve muscle-firing patterns that more closely approximate the movements of running and pedaling. The role of single-joint exercises for the cyclist is to improve the strength of a muscle group that is unusually weak and susceptible to injury.

If you continually develop your cycling skills, you will train your muscles to fire and relax at the right times, but only if you pay attention to where your head, shoulders, arms, knees, feet, and various other body parts are. An overview of these skills can be found in *Companion* Chapter 13. Doing drills without paying close attention and making small, almost imperceptible, corrections is a waste of your time.

Muscular Balance

Because cycling involves straightforward, repetitive movements, it is possible for the human body to make exceptional muscular and nervous system adaptations to perform them economically and efficiently. Through several years of training, the serious cyclist becomes very good at them. But for the same reason, they can also be detrimental as a result of the imbalances and postural changes that can occur. The most likely downside is injury when the forward-moving muscles are overdeveloped and the lateral ones all but ignored.

Overcoming muscular imbalances due to cycling is difficult since you can't change your position on your bike very much, or the single-plane movements of your feet while attached to the pedals. But in the weight room you may include some lateral strength building exercises, such as side lunges, side step-ups onto a box, and leg abduction and adduction exercises, to help balance out your muscular development.

COMPLEX TRAINING

One of the most effective ways to build muscular power is with plyometrics, a form of exercise involving explosive movements, such as jumping over or onto a high box. Including such exercises in your weekly training routine can be quite effective; the problem is that it takes more time than most of us have available. When you're already riding and lifting weights, adding

FIGURE 14: Box Jump

one or two more workouts to the week is close to impossible. The answer is to combine plyometrics and weights into one session. This is known as "complex training."

Complex training not only saves time but also magnifies the benefit of the plyometrics. This is because lifting weights stimulates the nervous system to activate more muscle fibers for a few minutes following an exercise. And activating large numbers of muscle fibers during a plyometrics exercise means higher power generation. Combining the two disciplines into one workout radically improves power. This means less effort to ride at any given power output.

There's one complex exercise I've found to be very effective for improving power. It's a combination of hip extensions, plyometrics, and on-bike sprints. Here's how it's done.

1. Do one SM set of your favorite hip-extension exercise (squat, leg press, or step-up). An SM set entails 6–12 reps at 60 percent of your one-rep maximum. The speed of the lift should be moderate. Proceed immediately with box jumps.

2. Do 20 box jumps (Figure 14). Stand on the floor facing a sturdy box. The box should be as high as possible, but you should be able to jump onto it from a crouched position. Jump up, landing on the

box with both feet and then step down. Do *not* do these in rapid succession. Take your time stepping down. Recovery is critical to building muscle power. If you can't do 20, then you didn't recover sufficiently or the box was too high.

3.   Immediately after the last box jump go to a stationary bike and do five standing 30-second sprints at maximum effort with high resistance at a cadence of 60 to 70 rpm. Sit down and spin easily to recover for 60 seconds. If possible, use your road bike on an indoor trainer instead of a stationary bike.

4.   Do three sets of the above, alternating between hip extensions, box jumps, and bike sprints.

This complex training session is best done in the Base 2 period eight to twelve times over four to six weeks.

Note: **Chapter 13 (Stretching) does not include any new material, so it does not appear in this *Companion*.**

14: Unique Needs

T he *Training Bible* covers the unique needs of athletes in particular categories: women, juniors, and masters competitors. The masters category is important because there are hundreds of masters in the world of sport who are within seconds or inches of their best performances of all time. What just 20 years ago was a young man's sport has become a sport for both sexes and all ages. I've added some considerations for both older cyclists and those just starting out.

CYCLISTS OVER 60

In recent years the masters category has grown to include very capable cyclists over the age of 60. The good news is that most members of this age category are patient and wise. They see cycling as a lifestyle, not as something to be defeated and vanquished. They're in it for the long haul. Younger athletes could learn a lot from them. If science could figure out how to put a grand master's wisdom into the mind of a 25-year-old physical specimen, it would create the ultimate athlete.

Whereas 40-something athletes can still make training mistakes and their bodies may well adapt and forgive them, riders over 60 have to be more careful to avoid pitfalls. This means getting the details exactly right for nutrition, rest and recovery, strength training, volume, intensity, equipment, and everything else that affects health and performance. Errors in

CYCLIST'S
TRAINING BIBLE
3rd ed.

See pp. 178–183
for more on
Masters Athletes

judgment at this age can mean unusable joints, surgery, broken bones, and, at the very least, days lost to lingering fatigue.

There are hundreds of masters in the world of sport who are within seconds or inches of their best performances of all time.

How should the grand master and the senior athlete train? All of the guidelines for masters athletes in the *Training Bible* also apply to the over-60 age group—only more so. To remain in top shape and to continue racing, they need to continue to challenge the muscular system, in particular. This means that strength training, hill work, and high-intensity efforts must be included regularly, yet spaced widely enough to allow for recovery. Strength training is especially important, and great gains can be made that will benefit not only the older rider's cycling but also his or her life in general. Research with 90-year-olds has found that their rate of improvement in strength is the same as that of 20-year-olds when they are put on a similar resistance-training program. By this age, cycling skills should be well-honed. If not, the risk of injury is magnified.

CYCLIST'S
TRAINING BIBLE
3rd ed.

*See p. 184 for
Acidic and Alkaline
Foods*

Nutrition must emphasize alkaline-enhancing foods in the vegetable and fruit categories. The older we are, the more likely we are to have acidic body fluids, which ultimately mean the loss of muscle and bone. In the *Training Bible* you'll find a table that ranks the acidity or alkalinity of common foods.

NOVICES

Whatever your age, if you have been cycling seriously for less than three years, you are considered a novice. Whatever your reason for accepting the challenge of bicycle racing, it's important for you to know the ingredients for success, especially those that are central to the sport. As with all sports, success in cycling, no matter how it's measured, is only as great as your preparation. Training must steel you to the specific demands of the goal event. For example, a hilly course requires training in the hills, and long races demand great aerobic endurance. In fact, endurance is the single most important requirement of the sport regardless of the race. If you can't go the distance, nothing else matters.

Training to Go the Distance

If pressed, most riders will admit that they like training more than racing. Races are merely the carrot on the stick that gets them on the road as soon as they get home from work. Without races, there would be no feeling of necessity or sense of urgency about workouts. Races give focus and direction to training. Workouts, however, are the fun part. That's when you can drop all of the cares of the day and concerns for tomorrow, while living strictly in the present. Riding a bike reduces life to its most basic elements—breathing and movement.

Workouts are also when you may get together with your team or training partners who share common interests. Having partners to train with makes the effort seem easier and boosts motivation. And there will certainly be times when motivation wanes. Even the best in the sport find their desire to work out has highs and lows. This is not a sign of weakness, and may even have self-protection benefits, such as ensuring recovery. But too many workouts missed due to low enthusiasm means erosion of fitness and poor race performance. It is at such times that a training group is most beneficial. So find some other riders who want to do some of the same kinds of rides you are interested in doing—possibly through a local cycling club or by putting the word out for training partners through a local bike shop—and schedule your week to regularly work out with them.

> A common mistake that novices make is to bring too much motivation to the sport. A conservative approach to training is critical in the early stages of your fitness development.

A common mistake that novices make is to bring too much motivation to the sport. Compulsive training is likely to prevent you from achieving goals as it frequently leads to injury, illness, burnout, and overtraining. Chapter 2 presented an argument for training with moderation in a sport that appears, at least on the surface, to be extreme at times. At no time in your cycling career is a conservative approach to training more critical than in the early stages of your fitness development. Training with excessive volume and intensity at this time is counterproductive.

So how do you determine what is appropriate? Here are some tips that may provide guidance in your first year of training:

Volume. Are there externally imposed limits on the amount of time you have available to train? For example, if you realistically examine your workday and all other commitments, you may find that it is possible to fit in only one hour each day on the bike, perhaps even less. The weekends probably offer the most time for training. Winter brings fewer daylight hours and foul weather, further reducing training time.

Add up your available weekly hours using a conservative estimate, and multiply by 50 to find your projected annual training volume. This assumes that two weeks will be lost during the year to unavoidable illness, travel, or other commitments. The number you come up with includes all training time in addition to cycling, such as weight lifting, cross-country skiing, running, and any other crosstraining. Round off your annual hours to the closest 50 hours.

CYCLIST'S
TRAINING BIBLE
3rd ed.

See pp. 111–114 for
more on Weekly
Training Hours

Use Chapter 8 of the *Training Bible* to find a suggested periodization plan for your volume. You may find that it is necessary to slightly increase the lighter training weeks or decrease the high-volume weeks if your restrictions are imposed more by available time than by your physical capacity for training and recovery. Remember that Table 8.5 of the *Training Bible* is merely a suggested guideline, not a requirement.

CYCLIST'S
TRAINING BIBLE
3rd ed.

See pp. 95–97 for
more on the Base
Period

Periodization. In the first year of bike racing, it's best to train primarily in the Base periods as described in Chapter 7 of the *Training Bible*. This means you will focus on the development of aerobic endurance, force, technique (speed skills), and muscular endurance. These are the most important and basic components of bike-racing fitness and will take a year, possibly more, to hone. There is no reason to build power and anaerobic endurance, the other fitness components, before the basics are well established.

Weekly routines. There are endless possibilities for organizing your training week depending on time available, work schedule, experience with riding a bike, ability to recover, established group workouts, the times when a weight room is open, and numerous individual lifestyle issues. There is no standard way to arrange the week's workouts. Most new cyclists find, however, that doing one workout a day, plus a weekly day off, produces good results.

Weights. If you have only a few hours to train each week and it is difficult to fit everything in, weight workouts are the first ones to omit so that you may concentrate available time to the bike. Your greatest need at this stage of training is aerobic fitness. If you have time for the gym, and weight

Training Safety

Training for bike racing involves taking risks. Some of the risks you take may even be life-threatening, but you can minimize them by taking certain precautions. For example:

- Always wear a helmet when riding a bike.
- Avoid heavily trafficked areas whenever possible when riding.
- Ride only with safe groups while avoiding groups that run stop signs, ride in traffic, and generally do not obey traffic laws.
- Do not take undue risks on steep descents while riding.
- Make sure your bike is safe before starting a ride by testing your brakes, checking the quick releases to make sure they are tight, examining the tires to see if they have any cuts or show signs of too much wear, and tightening any loose bolts.

Also, if you experience any unusual physical conditions, such as chest pain, radiating arm or neck pain, an unusually high or erratic heart rate, joint soreness, back pain, unusual muscle or tendon discomfort, or blood in the urine, be sure to inform your doctor right away. Such conditions should also cause you to stop the workout immediately. Safety always comes first when riding a bike.

training doesn't compromise your on-bike training, use only the Anatomical Adaptation (AA) and Maximum Transition (MT) phases, as discussed in Chapter 12 of the *Training Bible*. Concentrate first on perfecting your technique with light weights. You will probably be surprised at how strong you become by doing just this. In the second full year of weight training, you can introduce the other strength-building phases.

Skills

As a newcomer to the sport of road racing, one of your greatest challenges in the first year will be developing and refining your bicycle skills. Riding with and observing experienced riders with good skills will help you hone yours. The starting point for building skills is getting your bike adjusted correctly by a professional fitter. Once your machine is properly fitted to your body and particular needs, the two basic skills of pedaling and cornering will be much easier to learn.

Pedaling cadence. Economy in riding a bike is based on an interaction between a human and a machine. How well they fit together is a significant determining factor in selecting an economical cadence. For example, short crankarms favor pedaling at a high cadence, whereas a high saddle position slows the cadence.

The cadence you use determines how you will feel in a race and how effectively you ride. Low cadences, for example, put stress on the knees and muscles and require greater muscular force generation than high cadences. High cadences require great metabolic effort, which causes heavy breathing. This means that a high cadence minimizes muscle fatigue but may cause you to use more energy, at least until you are better adapted to the level of activity.

Work on cadences as low as 60 rpm when climbing and as high as 120 rpm when sprinting.

Observations of elite riders reveal a common cadence range of about 90 to 100 rpm. This range is also supported by much of the recent research. Studies dating back to 1913 have shown the most economical cadence to vary from 33 to 110 rpm. Recent, more sophisticated studies, however, have tended to favor higher cadences, at least when self-selected by accomplished riders.

The bottom line is that pedaling at a cadence in the range of 90 to 100 rpm on a flat course is probably best. If you typically turn the cranks at a slower rate than this, you should spend your first year focusing on cadence drills to improve your economy. Work on cadences as low as 60 rpm when climbing and as high as 120 rpm when sprinting.

Cornering. Cornering is both a safety and a performance issue. The most common cause of bicycle crashes is poor cornering skills. Improving your cornering skills will help you to maintain a position in the peloton on a course with lots of turns.

As you can see in Figure 15, there are three ways to handle your bike when cornering—leaning, countersteering, and steering.

The *leaning method* is the most common technique used by novice cyclists regardless of the cornering situation. But it is really best when making a wide, sweeping turn on dry, clean pavement. In the United States and other countries where drivers and cyclists ride on the right side of the road,

FIGURE 15: Bicycle Cornering Techniques

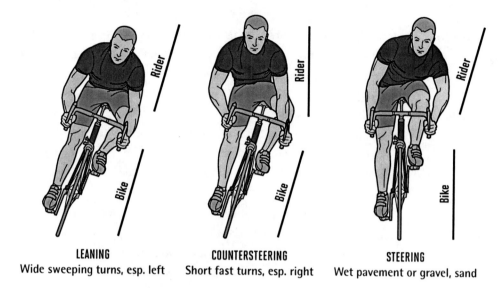

LEANING	COUNTERSTEERING	STEERING
Wide sweeping turns, esp. left	Short fast turns, esp. right	Wet pavement or gravel, sand

it is most effective when turning left. For those countries where drivers and cyclists ride on the left, this is the preferred right-turn method. To use the method, simply lean both the bike and your body into the turn with your weight on the outside pedal. If it is truly a wide, sweeping turn, you may be able to continue pedaling.

Few new to the sport use the *countersteering technique*, but it is quite effective for tight turns, such as right-hand turns in ride-on-the-right countries and left-hand turns in ride-on-the-left countries. Countersteering will get you around the corner with a much tighter radius than the leaning method will.

If you've learned countersteering on a motorcycle, the technique is the same. You must stop pedaling as you enter the turn because the bike tilt will be greater than with the leaning method. The inside pedal is up and your body weight is fully on the outside pedal. Here's where it feels counterintuitive: Straighten your arm on the inside of the turn and bend the elbow on the outside of the turn. It seems backwards, as you're pushing on the opposite handlebar that you would use for a sweeping turn—in fact, you're actually steering the bike out from under you. This motion breaks the gyroscopic effect of the turning wheels and causes you to lean the bike sharply into the turn as your body stays upright. You will go around the corner on a tight radius. In order for this technique to be effective, your speed must be at least 15 miles per hour (24 kph) or so. It takes practice to make it habitual.

Use the *steering method* when cornering on wet pavement or when there is sand or gravel on the road surface. Regardless of whether this is a right or left turn, you will need to slow down. If it is a tight-radius turn, such as a right turn in the United States, you must also stop pedaling. The purpose is to safely get around the corner without falling. The proper method involves keeping the bike upright while leaning only your body into the turn. Keep both knees near the top tube of the bike—do not point your knee at the corner.

When riding on wet pavement, reduce your tire pressure by about 25 percent. This will have minimal effect on your overall speed but will provide better traction in corners. The type of tire you use also plays a role when cornering. Tubular tires, also called "sew-ups," corner better than clinchers, as they have round sidewalls, whereas clinchers have flatter sidewalls. Be especially careful when cornering on wet pavement if there is a painted stripe on the road. When wet, these are like riding on ice. The same goes for utility-hole covers—they are extremely slippery when wet. Use extreme caution when cornering on wet pavement on steep descents. Apply your brakes well before you get to the corner to reduce speed. Do not use the brakes when cornering.

Whether you are a novice or a masters athlete, there is not one formula for training derived from your age, experience, gender, or ability. It's just one of the reasons why coaching remains a fun challenge for me after so many years. It's my hope that what I've learned through experience will help you make the necessary modifications to your training so you can enjoy cycling even more.

15: Using a Training Diary

How can you determine what constitutes the optimum training method for your unique needs? Race results and testing can help because they are fairly objective measures of how you're doing. But these methods do not explain the causes of your performance improvements or declines. Fortunately, there is another way: Often, the causes can be discovered in your training records. Keeping a journal is your third most important task when not working out. It ranks right behind eating and resting.

Chapter 15 of the *Training Bible* covers how to plan with and use a training diary. Once you have recorded enough data, there are various ways to analyze it to find the strengths and weaknesses in your training approach.

CYCLIST'S
TRAINING BIBLE
3rd ed.

See pp. 191–198 for more on Planning with a Training Diary

ANALYSIS SOFTWARE

There are now many computer software programs available to help you analyze the data downloaded from devices such as power meters, heart rate monitors, and GPS units. The manufacturers of these training tools nearly always include their own software with the purchase of the device. Some of the programs that come in the box are quite basic but others are fairly elegant.

The problem with most of the software that comes with these devices is that it was designed by a company that makes excellent hardware but knows little about software. Unfortunately, the manufacturer rarely knows what's important in training either. Aftermarket training-analysis software designed by knowledgeable athletes in a software-focused company is usually better than the software that comes with the product.

One of the best software-analysis tools is called "WKO+" and is available online at Trainingpeaks.com. I admit I'm biased as I've played a small role in developing the software and use it to analyze all of my clients' training and racing. The reason I use it is that it is a powerful tool for the serious athlete and makes for easy analysis of almost any training device you own. It works with heart rate and power data regardless of your device's manufacturer, as long as the device comes with a cable or wireless capability for uploading information to a computer.

You should be able to figure out whether you are improving, and exactly how much you are improving.

No matter what software you use, the key question it should help you answer is whether you are making progress toward your racing goals. By using the software, you should be able to figure out whether you are improving, and exactly how much you are improving. If the software doesn't easily help you do this, then it is useless. Make sure the software you are using offers these functions:

- Calculates the time you have spent in each heart rate and power zone by workout and for the entire season
- Indicates when you are ready to change your zones in training as a result of fitness changes
- Supplies a way for you to easily compare similar workouts
- Calculates changes in power relative to body weight
- Records improvements in workout power for similar workouts
- Predicts your capacity for handling greater training stress
- Estimates the level of fatigue you can manage without breaking down
- Provides a graphic or metric that shows how your fitness is progressing
- Includes a way of determining when you are ready to race

CYCLIST'S
TRAINING BIBLE
3rd ed.

*See pp. 198–199
for more on
Analysis*

Even if you decide to use software to help you interpret your training data, it can still be incredibly useful to keep a diary. If the hard-copy approach provided in the *Training Bible* doesn't work for you, there are plenty of electronic formats that might suit you better. Regardless, a diary helps you see the big picture by keeping all the details in focus, both the hard data and the subjective feedback. When used effectively, it serves as an excellent tool for planning your steps, motivating you, and diagnosing your problems. It also provides a personal history of training and racing accomplishments. A well-kept diary ranks right up there with training, rest, and nutrition when it comes to developing a competitive edge.

CYCLIST'S
TRAINING BIBLE
3rd ed.

See Figure 15.1 and pp. 262–263 for a sample diary and template

16: Fuel

How and what should you eat to maximize performance now and for many healthy years to come? The possibilities are nearly endless—and endlessly confusing. In this chapter I discuss the cyclist's nutritional needs and how to meet those needs.

THE FIVE STAGES OF RECOVERY

It is well established that carbohydrates are necessary for high levels of performance in endurance sports such as bike racing. Just as critical to success is the timing of carbohydrate intake. In fact, if your carb intake is timed correctly, you can actually cut back a bit on the amount and take in a wider variety of nutrient-dense foods. Those foods can in turn help you recover faster and perform at a higher level.

> If your carb intake is timed correctly, you can take in a wider variety of nutrient-dense foods, which can help you recover faster and perform at a higher level.

First, accept that your workouts are the central events of each day, and that the types of foods you eat and when you eat them are determined by workout timing. This is likely a fairly easy notion to acquire since, as a serious athlete, you probably already have a "training is life, everything else is just the details" way of seeing the world.

Each workout has five feeding times linked with it. I call these "stages." Here's how they work.

Should You Hyperhydrate?

The day before a race, it's common to see athletes walking around with bottles of water or sports drink. Is this a good idea? Does taking in a large volume of water prevent dehydration the next day? The answer is no. If you were a camel with a large reservoir designed just for holding excess water as you trudged across the desert, excessive drinking would be beneficial. But since you are reading this you are more than likely a human. We don't have a spare tank to fill. Once our limited storage areas are full, most of the excess is shunted to the bladder and removed as urine. If that's all that happened, hyperhydration would not be much of a problem. But it's not.

Excessive drinking has been shown to dilute the body's electrolyte stores, especially sodium. So excessive water intake is likely to increase your risk of hyponatremia. This is a condition in which sodium stores are too low and the body begins to shut down. In the early stages you may experience nausea, headache, muscle cramps, weakness, and disorientation. In the latter stages, seizures and coma are possible.

Although hyponatremia is unlikely to occur in races that take less than about four hours, it simply isn't a good idea to start any race, regardless of distance, with diluted electrolytes. Pay attention to your thirst mechanism. We've been taught that it is not effective and that we shouldn't trust it, but that's an old wives' tale. Drink when you are thirsty. It's that simple.

CYCLIST'S
TRAINING BIBLE
3rd ed.

*See pp. 212–213
for more on
Periodization
of Diet*

Stage 1—Before the Workout

The goal of this stage is to store sufficient carbohydrates to get you through the workout. This is especially important for early-morning rides. For the perfect fuel, eat 200 to 400 calories, primarily from a moderate-glycemic-index, carbohydrate-rich food, two hours before the workout. Of course, few are willing to get up at 4 a.m. just to eat before a 6 a.m. ride. For these early-morning sessions, especially races and highly intense rides, try downing a bottle of your favorite sports drink or a couple of gel packets with 12 ounces of water about 10 minutes before the workout. This isn't quite as good as eating a real breakfast two hours beforehand, but it is far better than training on a low fuel tank.

Stage 2—During the Workout

For an hour or less of training, water is all you need, assuming you refilled the tank in Stage 1. For longer workouts you also need carbohydrates, mostly in the form of liquids from a high-glycemic-index source. The best choice is your favorite sports drink. You could also use gels, chased immediately by lots of water. The longer the workout, the more important the carbohydrate is and the more of it you need. You'll need as few as 120 calories or as many as 500 calories per hour, depending not only on workout length but also on your body size, workout intensity, and level of experience. It's usually a good idea for this liquid fuel source to include sodium, especially if it's a hot day and you tend to sweat heavily. The research is less than overwhelming on other ingredients of sports drinks and gels, including potassium, magnesium, and protein. Include them if you want to. If you pay careful attention as you train and experiment with your nutrition, you can develop a sense of the type of carbohydrate that works best for you and the amount you need for different workouts.

Stage 3—Immediately After the Workout

This and the next stage are the key times in the day for taking in carbohydrates. When athletes say that eating in stages, as described here, doesn't work for them, it's usually because they don't take in enough carbohydrates in Stages 3 and 4.

Your goal in Stage 3 is to replace the carbohydrates you used up during the workout. In the first 30 minutes or so after a workout, your body is several hundred times more sensitive to carbohydrates and will readily store more than at any other time of the day. The longer you wait to refuel, the less likely you are to completely refill the gas tank. Take in three to four calories per pound of body weight, mostly from carbohydrates, in this stage.

You can buy a commercial product for this type of refueling, but most are expensive. You can make your own refueling concoction by blending the following ingredients:

16 ounces of fruit juice

1 banana

3–5 Tbsp. glucose (such as Carbo-Pro, available at sportquestdirect.com), depending on body size

2–3 Tbsp. protein powder (egg or whey sources are best)

2–3 pinches of salt

Consuming this drink during the 30-minute, post-workout window is critical for recovery. It should be your highest priority after a hard workout. If the workout lasted less than an hour and was low intensity, omit this stage.

Stage 4—As Long as the Workout Lasted

Continue to focus your diet on carbohydrates, especially from moderate- to high-glycemic-index sources, along with some protein, for a time period equal to the amount of time you were working out. You may be ready to eat a meal during Stage 4 if the workout was long. Now is the time to eat low- to high-glycemic-index starches such as pasta, bread, bagels, cereal, rice, and corn to facilitate the recovery process. Perhaps the perfect foods to eat at this time are potatoes, sweet potatoes, yams, and bananas, since they also have a net alkaline-enhancing quality that reduces body acidity following workouts. Raisins are a great snack food for Stage 4. Eat until satisfied.

Stage 5—Until the Next Workout

Usually, by the time Stage 5 comes around, you will be at work, back in class, spending time with your family, mowing the grass, or doing whatever it is you do when not training or racing on a given day of the week. Although this part of your day may look ordinary to the rest of the world, it really isn't. You can still focus on nutrition for long-term recovery.

This is the time when many athletes get sloppy with their diets. The most common mistake is to continue to eat Stage 3 and 4 foods that are low in nutrient value and high in starch and sugar. Such foods are great for post-workout recovery but relatively poor in vitamins and minerals. The most nutrient-dense foods are vegetables, fruits, and lean protein from animal sources, especially seafood. Or you can snack on nuts, seeds, and berries. These are all good foods for Stage 5. They are all rich in vitamins, minerals, and other trace elements necessary for health and growth.

Avoid processed foods that come in packages, including those with labels that say "healthy." They aren't, and that even includes foods invented by sports nutrition scientists. They are still several million years behind nature in producing nutritious chow. Just eat *real* food in Stage 5.

Diet and Reality

The Italians have a knack for living the good life, and with the help of a famous Italian economist, there's a way to apply *la dolce vita* to your training diet as well. The economist is Vilfredo Pareto, who in 1906 made the acute observation that 80 percent of the land in Italy was owned by 20 percent of the population. Experts in other fields soon discovered that Pareto's "80-20 rule" applied to their areas of study as well.

For example, 80 percent of the productivity in a business typically comes from 20 percent of the employees. Schoolchildren spend 80 percent of their time with 20 percent of their friends. Stock-market investors find that 80 percent of their income comes from 20 percent of their stock.

We can apply Pareto's Principle to our diets, too. The lesson is simply this: You don't need to eat perfectly. Stage 5 of recovery, where we spend most of our eating life, is often viewed as being quite restrictive. We're supposed to eat "the perfect diet," focusing on fresh fruits, steamed vegetables, and lean protein. Happily, the 80-20 Rule tells us that it's okay to occasionally eat a cookie, a slice of pizza, a piece of garlic bread, or even a bit of creamy fettuccine Alfredo—so long as this makes up less than 20 percent of your food intake. In other words, it's perfectly acceptable to cheat a little. Just make sure that 80 percent of the food on your plate in Stage 5 is nutrient-dense, and you will be healthy, lean, fit, and fast. Pareto's Principle: another reason cyclists can thank the Italians.

If you are doing two workouts or race stages in a day, you may not get to Stage 5 until late in the day. Also, Stage 4 may replace Stage 1 with closely spaced workouts. That's not a problem.

That's all there is to it—a simple way to organize your day into five stages of eating to ensure adequate recovery and optimal health. You can find more details on this topic in my book *The Paleo Diet for Athletes*.

BODY WEIGHT MANAGEMENT

Cyclists are often concerned with losing weight to improve climbing. There's little doubt that being lighter means going up hills faster. A pound of excess body weight takes about two watts to get up a hill. That doesn't sound like much, but what if you could shed 10 pounds of fat? For most riders, that would mean ascending a hill 7 to 10 percent faster. That is a significant improvement in performance that would otherwise take lots of sweat and months of hard training to accomplish.

Trying to cut weight when you are already close to your optimal size is not a good idea. The key is to figure out what your optimal size is.

Although there is no question that excess body weight is a great handicap in climbing, this is not to say that all cyclists should lose weight. Trying to cut weight when you are already close to your optimal size is not a good idea. The key is to figure out what your optimal size is.

A good way to think about your body weight is in comparison to your height. For example, a 200-pound cyclist would be quite skinny if he were 7 feet tall. Your weight-to-height ratio is a simple and much more effective way to think about body mass than relying solely on the bathroom scale.

Determine your ratio by dividing your weight in pounds by your height in inches. Men who are good climbers are generally less than 2.1 pounds per inch. High-performance women climbers are generally under 1.9 pounds per inch. Men who exceed 2.5 pounds per inch and women above 2.3 are best advised to find flat race courses where they have an advantage—particularly if the wind is blowing.

If you are above the climber weight-to-height-ratio range and you want to climb faster, what is the best way to drop those last few pounds? Unfortunately, studies on the best way for serious athletes to lose weight are rare. One group of researchers, however, has examined the issue in an interesting way. They compared eating less to exercising more to see which was more effective in dropping excess body fat.

The study followed six endurance-trained men who created a 1,000-calorie-per-day deficit for seven days. They did this in one of two ways, either by exercising more while maintaining their caloric intake, or by eating less while keeping exercise the same. The "exercise more" men added 1,000 calories of exercise daily—comparable to riding an additional 35 or so miles—and averaged 1.67 pounds of weight loss in a week. But the "eat less" men dropped 4.75 pounds on average for the week. Apparently, restricting food intake has a greater return *on the scales* than increasing the training workload does.

Notice that I said "on the scales." Unfortunately, the reduced-food-intake group in this study also lost a greater percentage of muscle mass than the increased-exercise group. That is an ineffective way to lose weight. If the scales show you're lighter, but you have less muscle to create power, the trade-off is not a good one.

How can you reduce calories and yet maintain muscle mass? Unfortunately, that question hasn't been answered for athletes. One study did address it for sedentary women, however. Perhaps the conclusions are still applicable to athletes.

In 1994, Italian researchers had 25 women eat only 800 calories a day for 21 days. Ten ate a relatively high-protein, low-carbohydrate diet. Fifteen ate a low-protein, high-carbohydrate diet. Both groups were restricted to 20 percent of calories from fat. The two groups lost similar amounts of weight, but there was a significantly greater loss of muscle for the women on the high-carbohydrate, low-protein diet.

So if cutting calories is more effective than increasing exercise for weight loss, it appears that the protein content of the diet must be kept at normal levels. This assumes that you're eating adequate protein before starting the diet, which many athletes aren't. If your protein intake is already low, typically less than about 20 percent of total calories, then dieting will negatively affect training quality and you are likely to lose muscle mass.

This leaves one question: When is the best time in the season to lose excess weight? When one of the athletes I coach needs to drop a few pounds, we try to accomplish this in the early Base period. The challenge for most athletes is that this generally includes the holiday season at year end. That can be a difficult time of year to reduce food intake. But by the time we reach Build 1—about 11 weeks before the first A-priority race—it's really too late. At that point we need to accept whatever his or her body weight is and move on to the more challenging race-like training.

17: Problems

With rare exceptions, the problems we face in training and racing are of our own making. Our motivation to excel is exceeded only by our inability to listen to our bodies. The result is often overtraining, burnout, illness, or injury. This chapter describes how to avoid these problems, or, if they haven't been avoided, how to deal with them.

RISK AND REWARD

Choosing your workout for the day is a lot like investing in the stock market. When buying stock, the wise investor considers the risks and rewards each stock offers. There are blue chip stocks, which have a very low risk but increase in value slowly and steadily over time. Then there are penny stocks, generally offered by smaller or newer companies and considered quite volatile and speculative. They are risky—but the potential reward is also quite high. So you can play it safe with blue chip investments, or risk everything on striking it rich with the right penny stock.

> **Our motivation to excel is exceeded only by our inability to listen to our bodies. The result is often overtraining, burnout, illness, or injury.**

Every workout you do has a similar risk/reward equation. Some workouts are low risk in terms of duration or intensity, but have a low return in terms of fitness. Others cost more in terms of your time and energy investment, but can allow your fitness to increase dramatically, particularly if you are wise enough not to overdo it.

FIGURE 16: Risk and Reward in Training

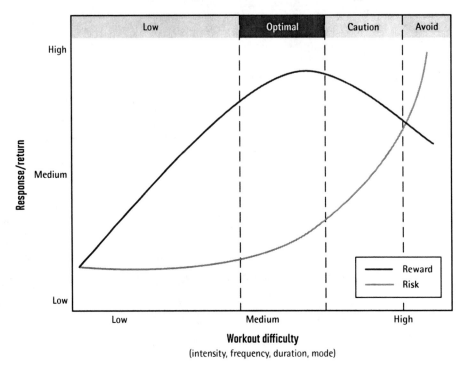

Workout difficulty
(intensity, frequency, duration, mode)

Note: A low degree of workout difficulty yields low to modest returns, but this range is the safest approach to training.

Finding the right ratio of risk to reward for breakthrough workouts requires a delicate balance between pushing yourself to new levels and allowing yourself to get adequate rest so that your body can recover properly. The risks associated with these potentially high-paying workouts are the aforementioned overtraining, burnout, illness, and injury. Training time is lost when these setbacks occur, and so the overly aggressive athlete must return to basic, low-risk, low-reward training to reestablish a previously attained fitness level. Athletes who experience these conditions frequently may be addicted to high-risk training. Figure 16 illustrates the workout risk and reward curves.

Risk is associated with the potential results from some combination of the frequency, intensity, duration, and mode of training and is unique for each athlete. What is high risk for one rider may be low risk for another. The difference has to do with experience, fitness levels, susceptibility to injury, previous training adaptations, age, and other factors.

Each athlete has a workout frequency and duration that is optimal. An elite cyclist may work out six hours a day for several days in a row and become more fit. But a novice trying to do this will soon break down and be forced to stop training for several days in order to recover. This is often referred to as "too much too soon." It's imperative that you find a workout frequency and duration that works for you and then stick to it.

The same holds true for the intensity of workouts. A lot of training done at high intensity, such as intervals, hard group rides, and races on consecutive days, makes for very risky but potentially rewarding training. If you survive it with your body and health intact, you will become a much fitter rider. Most can't safely sustain this level of training.

Whenever you work out for some period of time with high frequency, intensity, or duration, you must lower the risk by including substantial recovery time. Frequent recovery is the key to keeping this type of risk at a manageable level.

Risk associated with "mode" refers to the type of workout you do—including cycling, weight lifting, and crosstraining sports such as running and swimming. Of these modes, running is the riskiest because of the stress it places on bones and soft tissues. For some athletes, a lot of running is likely to cause injury; those who approach running cautiously, however—by strengthening their running-related tissues and bones gradually over a long period of time—may find that it produces good general aerobic conditioning, especially early in the training season.

Weight lifting also has the potential to be a high-risk mode of training. Going to high-load lifting before the body is ready can easily cause injury. I've seen it happen with many athletes who became too aggressive with the risks they took in the weight room.

Within a weight training regimen, some exercises are riskier than others. Freebar squats are a good example of this. A heavily loaded bar placed on the shoulders may be especially risky for the athlete who is new to the weight room, who has experienced knee or hip injuries, or who is an older athlete with degenerating spinal disks. But if you can handle it, the reward reaped from squats is significant. Leg presses, step-ups, and lunges are less risky exercises: They work most of the same muscle groups as squats, but also carry a lesser reward.

Plyometric exercises—explosive movements done to build power, as described in Chapter 12—also have the potential to be both high risk and high reward. Eccentric-contraction plyometrics are riskier but potentially more rewarding than concentric-contraction plyometrics. An example of an eccentric-contraction plyometric exercise is jumping off of a high box, landing on the floor, and then immediately springing back up to a second high box. A concentric-contraction version of this same exercise eliminates the jump down and landing, so you are simply jumping to the high box and stepping down. You'll find this exercise illustrated in *Companion* Chapter 12. There is less potential for reward this way, but also less risk.

The purpose of this chapter is to help you realize that when selecting a workout, you need to consider the reward you hope to get from it and the risks involved in doing it. By investing wisely in your training, you will increase your likelihood of building excellent fitness through consistency while avoiding the common pitfalls of overly aggressive training. If you make a mistake in your training, make it on the side of low risk rather than high risk. I guarantee you will do better in the long run.

TRAINING MISTAKES

It's amazing how often I see different athletes make the same mistakes. In fact, I've found that there are seven mistakes that are so common that nearly everyone makes them, from novice to experienced pro. I see it happen every season.

Mistake #1: No direction. Almost every athlete has goals, but there are two problems with the goals they most often set. First, they are usually too vague. The typical athlete makes "I want to get better" goals for which it is impossible to measure whether progress is being made. Second, the goals are usually forgotten when hard training or racing begins. Many athletes become so absorbed in preparing for the next race that they become myopic about training, focusing on the short term instead of the long term.

Mistake #2: No priorities. Without priorities, every race is treated as critical. It's easy to make this mistake, especially if you're doing a series of races that all count toward the final standings. Without priority races, you never have an opportunity to truly peak and can never fully realize what you're capable of doing in a race. That means permanent mediocrity.

Mistake #3: Training the wrong stuff. Most athletes have a pretty good idea of their weaknesses, but they don't work hard enough at correcting them. It's like the old saying, "A chain is only as strong as its weakest link." If your weak link is climbing, and the season's most important race is on a hilly course, you'd better be doing a lot to train yourself to climb better. Paying lip service to climbing while spending a lot of time and energy on flat courses, which you may enjoy more, won't do much to produce good race results. The weak link is still weak.

Mistake #4: Intervals too soon. I've never figured out why an athlete who doesn't have a race until May is out doing gut-busting intervals in December. Why are athletes so eager to start intervals? I hope you're not doing this, but chances are good that you are. Wait until later in the season.

Mistake #5: Not enough rest. This may be the most common mistake cyclists make. Nearly everyone who is even slightly serious about training ends up doing it sooner or later. I suspect it's so common because those who are successful in endurance sports tend to have certain personality traits. They learned at an early age that hard work produces results. So when things are going well, they work hard. And when things aren't going well, they work harder. In fact, they believe that hard work is the solution to all problems. This inevitably leads to overtraining (see mistake #6).

Mistake #6: Ignoring fatigue. Endurance athletes seem to believe they are Superman or Superwoman. Although they may understand that too much training and too little rest results in overtraining, they seem to think they are immune to the problem. When the signs of overtraining appear, they ignore them and continue as if they're just minor hindrances. "Overtraining can't happen to me" is the general belief.

Mistake #7: Not tapering for big races. Either athletes don't know how to taper for important races, or they're afraid of losing fitness by backing off. Every year I see athletes doing excessively long and hard workouts the week of an important race. They just don't understand that race-week rest is what will produce their best result on the weekend.

CYCLIST'S
TRAINING BIBLE
3rd ed.

*See pp. 228–232
for more on
Overtraining*

Preventing mistakes and planning to avoid problems is essentially what a coach does for you. Coaches know that if they can just hold an athlete back a bit, the race results will take care of themselves. You'll be a better self-coach by eliminating such errors.

18: Recovery

I n this chapter I will explain recovery, an important and often underrated aspect of training, more fully. Due to the nature of the sport, with its stage races and double-race weekends, cycling often requires the athlete to be ready to go again within a few hours. In addition, the sooner a cyclist can do another breakthrough workout, the sooner his or her fitness will improve. Recovery holds the key to both of these situations. We've discussed nutrition's five stages of recovery around strenuous workouts (see *Companion* Chapter 16), now it's time to focus on the role recovery plays in training, on a daily, monthly, and annual basis.

CYCLIST'S
TRAINING BIBLE
3rd ed.

See pp. 238–239 for more on The Need for Recovery

RECOVERY PERIODIZATION

If you could wish for one athletic-enhancing gene, it should be the one that improves your capacity to recover quickly from workouts. Athletes with this gene seem to naturally become the best athletes in their respective racing categories. This is a conclusion I've drawn from my own observations, and while there isn't any scientific data to back it up, there seems to be a strong correlation between one's ability to recover and the rate of one's fitness progression. Recovering quickly also means getting in good shape quickly.

Recovery plays an important role in training, on a daily, monthly, and annual basis.

Why is this so? There is an easy explanation: It's during recovery following hard training that the body realizes the changes that we call "form," which is simply to say that one's potential for performance in a race or in subsequent training develops during rest. These changes may result in fat-burning enzyme increases, more resilient muscles and tendons, decreases in body fat, greater heart stroke volume, enhanced glycogen storage, and so on. Besides overloading your body with the stresses of hard exercise, focusing on recovery is the most powerful thing you can do in training to perform at a higher level. But this is the part of the training process that most self-coached athletes get wrong. They don't allow for enough recovery, and consequently, they overwhelm their bodies with stress.

Let's look at where recovery figures into the Annual Training Plan you created in Chapter 8.

Yearly recovery. Recovery takes place during the Transition periods that come after the Race periods in your training plan. The purpose of these low-volume, low-intensity Transition periods is to allow your body and mind to rejuvenate themselves before you start back into another period of hard training. If you have two A-priority races in a season, you should generally have two Transition periods. The first may only be for three to five days, but the one that comes at the end of the season may well last for four weeks or more depending on the difficulty level of the previous season, especially the final part.

Monthly recovery. Build recovery into your monthly training plan every third or fourth week (more frequently for masters riders). This regular period of reduced workload may be three to seven days, depending on what you did in the previous hard training weeks, how fit you are becoming, how quickly you tend to recover, and other individual factors.

Figure 17 illustrates what happens when you schedule a monthly recovery time. As your fatigue increases over the course of two to three weeks of increasing workloads, your form diminishes. Form is your potential for performance. In other words, how well you may train or race at any given point in time is based on how rested you are. Notice that fatigue and form follow nearly opposite paths. A key principle of training is to unload fatigue frequently, which has the effect of improving your readiness to train and race well again. If you do not unload accumulated fatigue, you become a zombie struggling through low-quality workouts with no enthusiasm.

Weekly recovery. Within each week there should be hard and easy days. No one, not even elite athletes, can train hard every day with no recov-

FIGURE 17: Impact of Recovery on Fatigue and Form

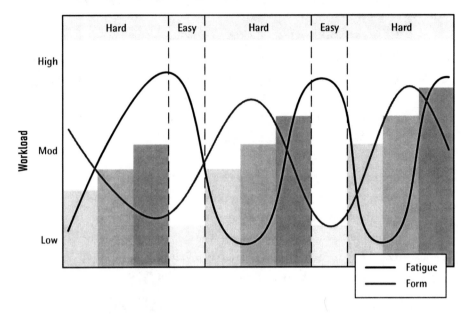

ery breaks. Just as with any part of training, "easy" is a relative term. Some athletes need a day completely off from exercise every week. Other athletes, especially those with the quick-recovery gene who also have a high capacity for work, can work out seven days a week. These elite athletes still need easy days each week, however. And even they need an occasional day off completely from exercise. A day off the bike not only aids physical recovery but mental recovery as well.

Daily recovery. When you are doing two-a-day workouts, there will be times when both are challenging sessions, but there will also be days when both are light workouts or one is hard and one is easy. This is what makes training so complex and why having a coach is often necessary to achieving high levels of success.

CYCLIST'S
TRAINING BIBLE
3rd ed.

See pp. 241–243 for more on Recovery Methods

How often you insert recovery into your training program, how long this period of recovery lasts, and exactly what recovery means to you in terms of workout duration, intensity, and frequency is an individual matter. The only sure way for you to know what will work best for you in terms of each of these factors is through trial and error. Some athletes will find they can

Ice Baths

Some cyclists find that ice baths speed recovery. After the cool-down, fill a tub halfway with cold water. Add a large bag of ice, climb in, and remain in the tub for 7 to 10 minutes. The water should cover your legs completely (this could be the most painful part of your workout!). In the absence of ice, you can alternate hot and cold water in a shower for the same time period.

recover quite nicely on short periods of infrequent recovery. Others will discover they need frequent long periods to recover adequately.

Be aware that the need for recovery is a moving target; it changes according to the total stress in your life and your fitness level. Be conservative when trying different recovery programs. "Conservative" in this case means erring on the side of too much recovery.

About the Author

Joe Friel has trained endurance athletes since 1980. His clients have included amateur and professional road cyclists, mountain bikers, triathletes, duathletes, swimmers, and runners. They have been from all corners of the globe and have included American and foreign national champions, world championship competitors, and an Olympian.

In addition to *The Cyclist's Training Bible*, he is the author of *Cycling Past 50*, *Precision Heart Rate Training* (coauthor), *The Triathlete's Training Bible*, *The Mountain Biker's Training Bible*, *Going Long: Training for Triathlon's Ultimate Challenge* (coauthor), *The Paleo Diet for Athletes* (coauthor), *Total Heart Rate Training*, and *Your First Triathlon*. He holds a master's degree in exercise science and is a USA Triathlon and USA Cycling coach certified at their highest levels.

He is also a columnist for *VeloNews* and *Inside Triathlon* magazines and writes feature stories for other international publications and Web sites. He is frequently interviewed as an authority on sports training by media such as the *New York Times, Outside* magazine, the *Los Angeles Times*, and other leading publications. In addition, he consults with national Olympic federations.

Joe speaks at seminars and camps around the world on training and racing for endurance athletes and provides consulting services for corporations in the fitness industry. Every year he selects a group of the brightest coaches with the greatest potential and closely oversees their progress as they advance into the ranks of elite-level coaching.

For more information on personal coaching, seminars, camps, developmental coach mentoring, certification of coaches in the Training Bible methodology, coaching symposia, and consulting, go to www. TrainingBible.com. There you will also find training plans, a blog, a newsletter, and other free resources that provide updates to the Training Bible methodology described in this book. For all of the tools necessary for effective self-coaching using the concepts of this book, including a "virtual coach," go to http://TrainingPeaks.com.

Joe Friel may be contacted with questions or comments via e-mail at jfriel@trainingbible.com.

CPSIA information can be obtained at www.ICGtesting.com
Printed in the USA
BVOW05s1527010315

389815BV00024B/318/P